STRATEGIES FOR WRITING CENTER RESEARCH

LENSES ON COMPOSITION STUDIES
Series Editors, Sheryl I. Fontaine and Steve Westbrook

Lenses on Composition Studies offers authors the unique opportunity to write for advanced undergraduate and beginning graduate students who are new to the discipline of Composition Studies. While the series aims to maintain the rigor and depth of contemporary composition scholarship, it seeks to offer this particular group of students an introduction to key disciplinary issues in accessible prose that does not assume prior advanced knowledge of scholars and theoretical debates. The series provides instructors of advanced undergraduate or beginning graduate students texts that are both appropriate and inviting for this fresh but professionally directed audience.

OTHER BOOKS IN THE SERIES
Composition Studies Through a Feminist Lens, by Shari J. Stenberg (2013)
Critical Conversations About Plagiarism, edited by Michael Donnelly, Rebecca Ingalls, Tracy Ann Morse, Joanna Castner Post, and Anne Meade Stockdell-Giesler (2013)
Bibliographic Research in Composition Studies, by Vicki Byard (2009)

Strategies for Writing Center Research

Jackie Grutsch McKinney

Parlor Press
Anderson, South Carolina
www.parlorpress.com

Parlor Press LLC, Anderson, South Carolina, USA

Printed in the United States of America

SAN: 254-8879

Library of Congress Cataloging-in-Publication Data

Grutsch McKinney, Jackie.
  Strategies for writing center research / Jackie Grutsch McKinney.
      pages cm
  Includes bibliographical references and index.
  ISBN 978-1-60235-719-8 (pbk. : alk. paper) -- ISBN 978-1-60235-720-4
(hardcover : alk. paper)
  1. Writing centers--Research--Methodology. 2. English language--Rheto-
ric--Study and teaching--Research--Methodology. I. Title.
  PE1404.G783 2016
  808'.042072--dc23
                              2015034196

                          1 2 3 4 5

Cover design by David Blakesley.
Printed on acid-free paper.

Parlor Press, LLC is an independent publisher of scholarly and trade titles
in print and multimedia formats. This book is available in paper, cloth and
eBook formats from Parlor Press on the World Wide Web at http://www.
parlorpress.com or through online and brick-and-mortar bookstores. For
submission information or to find out about Parlor Press publications, write
to Parlor Press, 3015 Brackenberry Drive, Anderson, South Carolina, 29621,
or email editor@parlorpress.com.

For Todd, Bennett, and Spencer

Contents

Acknowledgments

It wouldn't be wrong to say this is a book of evangelism—research evangelism, that is. I'm so thankful for all of those who inspired and enabled me to spread the word.

The seed was planted by by Becky Jackson and Elizabeth Chiseri-Strater who introduced me to qualitative inquiry and methods. Their classes, mentorship, and friendship opened new worlds of inquiry for me; I learned how to ask different questions, design studies, and how to listen closely to data for answers.

A big thanks is due to the awesome scholars who contributed to this book: Amber Buck, Nikki Caswell, Becky Jackson, Laurel Raymond, Karen Rowan, and Emily Standridge. Thank you for saying yes and pulling back the curtain on your research process.

At Ball State University, I get the privilege to work with many students on their theses, dissertations, and other research projects. I've learned immensely from sitting shotgun as students confront issues of study design, data collection, analysis, and representation. I thank all of the students over the years who have invited me along on the ride; I would not have had the confidence to write this book without the insights gained from observing your work.

I'm very glad that this book found a home at Parlor Press under the thoughtful direction of David Blakesley and the Lenses on Composition Studies series editors, Sheryl Fontaine and Steve Westbrook, who provided enthusiasm and spot-on revision suggestions throughout the process. Likewise, appreciation goes to colleagues and friends, near and far, who read chapters along the way and were faithful cheerleaders for the project from the start.

Finally, I thank my little family—Todd, Bennett, and Spencer—who don't care a lot about writing center research methods (yet!) but love me in a way that inspires me to do my thing.

Introduction

At the ripe age of twenty-two and a half as I entered my master's program in Rhetoric and Composition, I was awarded a graduate assistantship, which required me to teach a section of first-year writing and to work in the campus writing center. Being twenty-two and a half, I had no idea what I was doing but also, luckily, little frame of reference to understand how underprepared I was. I did not know, for instance, what rhetoric was, really, beyond the dictionary definition that I looked up before I packed my bags and drove my little Ford Escort across the country with my cat to start grad school. I honestly didn't know anything about Rhetoric and Composition as a field—I had no prior introduction into its history, its origins, its political struggles, its key figures or theories, or its particular ways of making knowledge.

The shame of my ignorance was intense in the beginning. I remember meeting a good-looking graduate student in my first week I wanted to impress. He asked me who my favorite rhetorician was, and I had to change the subject because I was pretty sure I didn't know any. That same week, my graduate class on liberatory pedagogy began with the professor asking us to say why we signed up for the course as we introduced ourselves. I sank deeper and deeper in my seat as my fellow classmates revealed that they knew both what *liberatory* and *pedagogy* meant; I knew neither and was only enrolled in the class because my advisor said I should take it and there were open spots. I was anxious teaching in my first-year writing classroom, too; I followed the prescribed syllabus and hoped no one asked questions.

In this tense transitional semester, I questioned my decision to go to graduate school, to specialize in Rhetoric and Composition, and to teach at all. I wasn't sure what role or what purpose I had in any context. It wasn't until a month or two later when I gradually found a place to belong and a reason to stay: the writing center. In the writing center, I could see I was making a difference. When I talked to student writers, I could see how their writing would transform. On the writing center couches, I could lounge about and talk with colleagues about how to do things differently, how to do things better. In the writing center, tutors and students alike admitted what they didn't know. They admitted that they made mistakes. I was able to let go of my shame and begin to teach and learn in earnest.

For these reasons, even as I've since found many ways to belong to the field of Rhetoric and Composition and many ways in which I can see that my work matters, I've remained committed to writing center work. Over the years, I've met many others who are drawn to writing center work because, like me, it was an entry point into the field that welcomed them as full participants even though they were absolute beginners. I've also come to see that many—if not most—people who work in writing centers begin their work unfamiliar with the larger discipline of Rhetoric and Composition. Many may work in a center for several years while pursuing an entirely different field of study and career path; others find themselves in writing center work after completing degrees in other fields. As a result, writing centers are full of tutors and administrators with practical experience tutoring and doing writing center work, but many do not, just like I did not, know the ways of participating in Rhetoric and Composition research.

This book was written for me, the writing center tutor and graduate student at age twenty-two and a half, who was desperate to become a member of the field but not sure how to do that. This book was also written for my undergraduate and graduate tutors over the years who are students in philosophy, journalism, math, Japanese, linguistics, education, audiology, and so on who want to engage in writing center research during their time as tutors, even if their career paths won't necessarily follow mine. Likewise, this book is for my graduate students working on conference presentations, seminar papers, theses, and dissertations and needing an introduction (quickly!) into writing center research. Writing center administrators, too, who may or may not have a background in Rhetoric and Composition, will also be able to use this book for preparing their own research in and on writing centers and, importantly, mentoring their staffs in conducting writing center research. Finally, this book is for my colleagues in Rhetoric and Composition more broadly who may not be directly involved in writing center work but see the rich potential for the writing center as a research site. For them, this book can be a guide to key studies and established research practices in writing centers.

WHY CONDUCT WRITING CENTER RESEARCH?

My argument in writing this book on writing center research for these various audiences is that we need more research on and in writing centers. In arguing this, I'm joining a line of many other writing center scholars who have advocated the same thing over the course of many years (see North; Haswell; Boquet and Lerner). And, we can see evidence throughout the last few decades that scholars have answered that call—more scholarship is being produced on writing centers and in writing centers. For one example, ProQuest Dissertation and Thesis database lists eleven projects in the 1980s, seventeen projects in the 1990s, forty-eight projects between 2000 and 2009, and already thirty-eight projects in this decade with "writing center" in the title.

However, it is still true that the majority of scholarship published in writing center journals—*The Writing Center Journal, The Writing Lab Newsletter,* and *Praxis*—is not research in the way I'll use the term in this book. *Research* here refers to empirical research, meaning *planned inquiry with systematic data collection, analysis, and reporting.* Alternatively, I'll use *scholarship* when referring more broadly to ways of producing and communicating knowledge, including what I've called research, as well as practitioner and theoretical inquiry. In a recent analysis of IWCA (International Writing Center Association) article award winners from 1985 to 2007, Sarah Liggett, Kerri Jordan, and Steve Price find that only seven of the twenty-two articles are "research," similarly defined ("Makers" 111–12). Similarly, Dana Lynn Driscoll and Sherry Wynn Perdue's study of two decades of articles published in *The Writing Center Journal* found that only six percent of articles contained empirical research (25). Thus, we may be seeing more writing center scholarship but not necessarily an increase in research.

There are perhaps many reasons why more writing center scholarship is not empirical research. First, writing center studies and its larger home discipline, Rhetoric and Composition, are relatively new areas of scholarly work. Though composition courses have been a part of college students' required curriculum for over a hundred years and early writing centers began almost that long ago as well (see Carino), until the 1960s and 1970s, the teaching of writing in classrooms, in writing centers, or elsewhere was something that was done, not something that was studied. The last half century has seen an about-face as journals, conferences, and graduate degree programs in composition studies have multiplied rather rapidly. In comparison to many other areas of study in the contemporary university, then, composition studies is a relative newcomer, and it has only been in the last few decades that scholars in composition studies have articulated ways of making knowledge, including research-based inquiry. More than just being new, composition studies and composition scholars were stigmatized in the beginning. Research in composition (or on anything related to teaching) often did not "count" as research for theses and dissertations or for faculty publications.

What was true for Rhetoric and Composition in general was perhaps doubly true for writing centers. Writing center scholars were looked down upon even by their composition peers; graduate students were openly discouraged from writing theses and dissertations on writing centers to avoid being marketable only as a writing center director (which implied decades of withering away in a windowless basement far from any intellectual stimulation). Today, still, the majority of colleges and universities do not hire writing center directors with PhDs in Rhetoric and Composition or appoint them to tenure-track faculty positions (see Balester and McDonald), which suggests that those appointed to writing center administrative positions are not expected to be scholars or researchers. Likewise, very few graduate programs offer courses on writing centers despite the steady increase of graduate programs in Rhetoric and Composition across the US (see Jackson, et al.).

All of this is not to say that the majority of present-day scholarship is not valuable; writing center scholarship today is absolutely thought-provoking, engaging, critical, and rigorous. The majority of present-day scholarship, however, favors making knowledge through theoretical or practitioner arguments. This book aims to equip writing center researchers with another way of making knowledge—by conducting empirical research—to complement the existing work. There are countless reasons readers might want to engage in writing center research. Here are some of the reasons why I engage in writing center research:

Participate and Contribute to a Larger Conversation

As I suggested in my opening, researching in writing centers opens the door to fuller participation in the field of Rhetoric and Composition. Knowing how to research and how to report on that research means being able to understand the language of the wider academic discipline and knowing how to talk back. Beyond just the field of Rhetoric and Composition, many other fields draw on similar methods for research.

Interrogate Practice

Perhaps because so many of those who work at writing centers are engaged in the hour-by-hour act of teaching writers, many writing center researchers are typically very interested in studying tutoring practices. Research can reveal details that we don't see while in the act of teaching one-to-one or even when reflecting on it.

Make Better Decisions

Especially in my role as an administrator, but even in my role as a tutor, I've needed to make decisions about writing center work. Sometimes, of course, a decision has to be made by the end of the day or even on the spot. But sometimes, especially when we encounter an ongoing issue, we can choose to take time to investigate the issue in all of its complexity before acting. Planning a study and acting on our findings rather than our hunches is prudent.

Make Strong Arguments

Schools at every level are increasingly data driven—how many students pass a particular test, how many students are retained, how many students graduate in four years or at all. As the data is now often tied to dollars, writing centers ought to be in the practice of gathering their own data.

Complicate Received Narratives

Oftentimes when we read writing center scholarship, attend writing center conferences, or enter into discussions at writing center staff meetings or courses, we find that others have assumptions about writing center work that do not seem to represent our experiences. These assumptions, when they are held by a wide number, can become stories or narratives that are passed down as representative or true for all. (Sometimes this is called *lore*.) When we do research, we can systematically study these ideas to see if they hold up under scrutiny.

Gain Academic or Professional Cachet

No doubt, some of the readers of this book have not chosen to do writing center research but have been assigned to do it as a part of a class or training program. Others will feel the need to do research to get into graduate school, to get a job, or to get tenure or promotion.

Enjoy Your Work More (or Again)

Researching asks you to put on different glasses, so to speak. You look at things you may see everyday but in a different way. So even things as mundane as a writing center handout or a transcript of an online tutoring session can pique your curiosity when you look at it as a researcher. Often, after you look at something as a data point in a research study, you can no longer see it as mundane even long after the study has ended.

It is likely that you already have and you will discover other reasons for conducting writing center research.

READING STRATEGIES FOR WRITING CENTER RESEARCH

This book is divided into three parts that correspond, more or less, to the stages of a research project. Though the medium of the book tends to reinforce linear reading practices, your use of this book—and your research itself—will likely be recursive. For example, research typically begins with planning, so in Part I of this book you'll find an overview of writing center research, an introduction to key terms for research, a discussion of how to conduct secondary research in writing center studies, and advice on shaping a research proposal. However, you probably will not be able to make key decisions needed for planning a research study until you understand options for methods and options for analyzing and reporting your findings, which are discussed in the other parts of the book. Therefore, you are encouraged to read through and circle back to parts to get a sense of possibilities before proceeding with your research.

Part II corresponds to the second part of a research project: collecting data. Each chapter in Part II aims to help readers select appropriate research methods for their research questions. This book familiarizes readers with strategies of discourse analysis, interviewing, surveying, fieldwork, and action research. Each chapter includes a thorough description and definition of the strategy addressed including a discussion of the limitations, ethical challenges, and pitfalls to expect, as well as a description of the sort of data collected. Each chapter also points to examples from writing center scholarship to illustrate how particular strategies have been employed by writing center researchers. Though the chapter divisions in this section may suggest that each strategy is distinct from the other, in fact, many if not most studies use more than one strategy for collecting data, and some studies will actually use all of these strategies. Thus, it is probably worthwhile to read all of the strategy chapters before landing on any particular strategy for your project.

The third part of this book discusses approaches for analyzing and reporting your research. Chapter 7 focuses on systematic, rigorous, and ethical approaches to qualitative analysis, and Chapter 8 discusses different venues for reporting on research data: classroom reports or presentations, conference presentations, research articles, digital compositions, theses or dissertations, job talks, poster presentations, or internal reports to writing center staff, administrators, or students.

You will also notice scattered throughout this book additional components designed to help you better conduct writing center research. One is the "Research Notebook," which includes reflection on a collaborative writing center research project in progress. You'll see in this notebook the choices the collaborative team, which I'm a part of, had to make in our research, the obstacles we had to face, and some solutions we found. By opening our research notebook to you, I hope the research process will be more concrete. You'll find one entry for the Research Notebook at the end of each Part. The second component you'll notice is "After the Study" sections where you'll find advice from writing center researchers who have completed a study. Each of these follow a particular strategy chapter—the same strategy used by the researcher in her work. Thus, Laurel Raymond's reflections follow the chapter on discourse analysis since her study used discourse analysis. In soliciting scholars for this component, I looked particularly for those who conducted studies as students since I imagine many readers will also be students. The studies discussed in the After the Study pieces have each been published elsewhere and/or have been successfully defended as graduate projects, so each is publicly accessible. Additionally, throughout the chapters, you'll find key words in bold. Each of these words is defined within the chapter and then again in the glossary at the end of the book. Each strategy chapter also contains questions For Discussion, Reflection, and Action and a list of key Recommended Resources. (All cited sources appear in the Works Cited near the end of the book whether or not they've been included in the recommended resources.) At the very end of the book, I've included a few helpful documents in the Appendices.

My wish for this book is that it helps the ever-widening circle of writing center researchers grow as more and more people discover the rich potential of the writing center as a research hub—a site where writers and tutors meet over texts. In many ways, the writing center conference (also called a session, tutorial, appointment, or consultation) is the smallest, atomic bit of contemporary composition theory in practice. An onlooker could see and hear the ways in which the tutor talks about writing; the sorts of assignments that students write to; the technology, genres, and mediums that writers are asked to use and choose to use; the activities that foster writing instruction; the assumptions about academic writing from students and from tutors. All of the political, theoretical, social, spatial, technological, and practical debates about how a student becomes a better writer play out before our eyes, hour after hour. Though there are many other places where formal writing instruction, conversations about writing, conversations about teaching writing, writing, and revision happen, these activities are all always occurring in writing centers. The possibility of the writing center for serious, interesting, groundbreaking writing research cannot be overstated.

Strategies for Writing Center Research

Research is formalized curiosity. It is poking and prying with a purpose.
—Zora Neale Hurston, *Dust Tracks on a Road*

Part I

1 Getting Situated

As a beginning tutor, the writing center for me was a place of successes and failures, work and gossip, talking and listening, lore and scholarship, inquiry and reception of knowledge. As I became more involved in writing center studies, I found the field provided a similar atmosphere. At conferences and while reading and discussing writing center scholarship, I discovered discourses both challenging and reassuring. I've found over the years that Rhetoric and Composition and writing center studies are somewhat unique as there are several acceptable ways of making knowledge—some of which were familiar to me when I began working at a writing center and some that were not. This chapter will introduce you to three types of inquiry used most often by those in Rhetoric and Composition and writing center studies. Then, in the second half, this chapter provides a brief history of existent writing center empirical research. As such, this chapter will be less oriented toward how to do research and more toward giving you a map of the terrain.

In the Introduction, I noted that writing center studies was a part of a larger academic discipline, called Rhetoric and Composition, writing studies, composition studies, or sometimes just Composition.[1] Writing center studies—the pedagogies, theories, scholars, and research that comprise it—is very tightly intertwined with Rhetoric and Composition. Thus those readers familiar with writing studies will be a step ahead; the types of inquiry used in Rhetoric and Composition and writing center studies are the same, for example. However, as Beth Boquet and Neal Lerner assert in "After 'The Idea of a Writing Center,'" Rhetoric and Composition is becoming increasingly fragmented and those who work within one subdiscipline (e.g., writing center studies) are less likely to read and cite one another in other subdisciplines (e.g., computers and writing). Likewise, each subdiscipline converges and diverges with the larger mother discipline. In this chapter, then, you'll see places where I describe what writing center studies takes from writing studies (how it converges) and what it brings (how it diverges).

WAYS OF KNOWING

Rhetoric and Composition sits at the intersections of three different ways of knowing and making knowledge. First, given the historical home of Rhetoric and Composition within English departments, much writing scholarship relies on making arguments using reasoning and textual evidence, as this is the traditional way of making knowledge in literature. Literary critics make an argument using literary and theoretical texts. Sarah Liggett, Kerri Jordan, and Steve Price call this **theoretical inquiry**. For theoretical inquiry, a writer asserts a claim and finds texts (literary texts, historic, or critical in the case of literary research) that provide evidence for the claims. In Rhetoric and Composition, scholars engage in theoretical inquiry by conversing with other published scholarship in Rhetoric and Composition and related fields. As such, Harry Denny's *Facing the Center* is an example of theoretical inquiry. Denny uses theorist Kenji Yoshino's ideas on assimilation and accommodation to press readers to face how issues like race, sexuality, and gender intersect with writing center work.

Second, given that Rhetoric and Composition is what Joseph Harris calls "a teaching subject," it has also been influenced by educational approaches to knowledge-making. Educational approaches are often empirical, using similar approaches as social scientists (which will be explained next). Yet, there is also another type of inquiry coming from education, which Liggett, Jordan, and Price call **practitioner inquiry**. In this approach, those with first-hand knowledge on a topic use their own experiences as evidence for their claims. In Rhetoric and Composition, this often takes the form of a teacher recounting a poignant example from a class or a writing assignment. In writing center studies, practitioner inquiry often centers around a tutor or an administrator's experience working with students or working within the institutional setting. Practitioner inquiry is reflective; it happens after the fact as the scholar tries to make sense of what has occurred, using his or her experiences to illustrate a point. The beginning of Elizabeth Boquet's *Noise from the Writing Center* is an example of practitioner inquiry. She begins the book with a memo she received from a colleague about the writing center being too loud; she reprints the memo and reflects on this moment as a catalyst to her larger arguments about the role of writing centers.[2]

Third, conducting empirical (experimental, quantitative, and qualitative) studies has been a part of writing studies scholarship since the inception of the field in the 1960s. Writing scholars have been influenced by the methods of—and sometimes collaborate directly with—social scientists who make knowledge by gathering and reporting on their own data in systematic ways, such as through interviews, surveys, case studies, and ethnographies. Liggett, Jordan, and Price call this approach **empirical inquiry**. Richard Haswell calls this type of research "RAD" meaning replicable, aggregable, and data-supported research. I'll sometimes call this type of inquiry, for simplicity's sake, research. For example, in the Introduction when I defined research as *planned inquiry with systematic data collection, analysis, and reporting,* I was defining this type of inquiry. Nancy Effinger Wilson's chapter in *Writing Centers and the New Racism* is an example of empirical inquiry. Wilson surveys forty-one faculty members and 103 tutors to assess attitudes toward African American Language (AAL), finding that tutors were more "caustic and indignant" than faculty toward AAL usage (189).

Table 1. Liggett, Jordan, and Price's Types of Inquiry

Theoretical Inquiry	Uses secondary sources for evidence
Practitioner Inquiry	Uses author's own experience as evidence
Empirical Inquiry	Uses data collected and analyzed by the researcher as evidence

In sum, the types of inquiry can be distinguished by what counts as evidence (Table 1). Yet, although I've presented these types of scholarship as though they are distinct categories, they aren't. It's common for a single piece of scholarship to combine types of evidence. That is, it is pretty typical for a scholar in an empirical study to also use theoretical analysis or personal experience in making an argument. In fact, the scholarship I've mentioned in this section—Denny's *Facing the Center,* Boquet's *Noise from the Writing Center,* and Wilson's "Bias in the Writing Center"—each defy singular categorization. Thus, when thinking about types of inquiry, you might ask yourself which is the primary type of evidence provided when categorizing the type of inquiry.

Though each of these approaches to scholarship is valid and produces valuable insights, it is only the last approach, empirical inquiry, that occupies the attention in this book. Focusing on empirical research might imply that the other types are not important, but this is hardly my intention. Instead, as recent important studies (Liggett, Jordan, and Price; Haswell; and Driscoll and Perdue) all attest, scholars in Rhetoric and Composition, and writing center studies in particular, publish very few empirical research studies compared with theoretical or practitioner inquiries. As mentioned in the Introduction, Liggett, Jordan, and Price find that fewer than one-third of all IWCA award-winning articles contain empirical research ("Makers" 112), and Driscoll and Perdue's study of articles published in *The Writing Center Journal* found that only six percent of articles contained empirical research (25). These numbers are shockingly low, especially given that writing center scholars often hope to engage with scholars across Rhetoric and Composition and across the disciplines. Empirical research—research that is data driven—is, typically, the *lingua franca* of the university. To participate fully in the scholarly exchange, writing center scholars need to conduct more empirical research and understand how to read and evaluate empirical research. My focus in this book on empirical research, then, is an argument for more empirical research. It stems from a recognition that many who wish to study writing center work might not have much, if any, background in empirical research practices. Further, those who come to writing center work from diverse backgrounds might not have the grounding in Rhetoric and Composition needed to understand the nuances of empirical researching in writing.

Types of Empirical Research: Qualitative, Quantitative, Mixed Method, and Experimental

For empirical writing center research, knowledge is made by clearly defining a study in advance of data collection, by systematically collecting and analyzing the data, and by fairly representing findings. The belief of researchers employing empirical research methods is that we can learn something about the world by careful study of small parts of it. Research is generally divided into two main types: qualitative and quantitative. **Qualitative research** uses words as its data and might be conducted within the natural setting, where the studied event or people naturally are. Interviews and ethnographies are two common approaches to qualitative research. Data collection for qualitative studies can continue for a semester, a year, or, in some cases, several years. Qualitative studies typically have fewer participants, but researchers learn more about them. **Quantitative research** use numbers for data and is typically collected by unobtrusive means, such as by survey or by **corpus**. Quantitative researchers do not typically need to go to their participants' settings. The data collection period for quantitative studies is usually, but not always, much briefer than qualitative studies. Quantitative studies may have hundreds or thousands of participants or data points.

Historically, proponents of one type of research were suspicious of the other. Quantitative researchers thought qualitative research relied on samples sizes that were too small and were not objective (enough) in analysis of data. Qualitative researchers felt that quantitative researchers hid behind guises of objectivity and over-relied on numbers to analyze and report complex human activities. Though you can still find entrenched members of each research type, nowadays most academics concede that the different types of research are both valuable, each type being appropriate for different types of questions.

Many researchers, in Rhetoric and Composition and writing center studies in particular, draw on both types of research within one project, a tactic that's called a **mixed-method approach**. That said, qualitative research is more often employed as the primary or dominant approach in Rhetoric and Composition because it is better suited to investigate the complex human activities involved in writing and the teaching of writing. In their study of empirical writing center research in *The Writing Center Journal,* Driscoll and Perdue find that sixty-three percent of studies used qualitative data, thirteen percent used quantitative data, and seventeen percent used a mixed-method approach (27–28). Thus, you'll find in this book that I give more attention to qualitative methods, but quantitative research methods are still touched on.

A third type of research called **experimental research** was popular in the 1960s and 1970s in writing studies. In experimental studies, the researcher manipulates the environment for the participants, resulting in either or both qualitative and quantitative data. In true experiments, the participants are divided into two or more groups; at least one group is given a **treatment** and at least one group is not (this group is called the **control group**). The fervor of experimental research for composition has cooled as scholars in rhetoric and composition placed more and more attention on the importance of context in writing. Experimental research (and its cousin quasi-experimental research) is used infrequently today in writing studies and writing center studies because controlling variables in a complex social activity like writing is very difficult, applying a treatment to some participants and not others might have ethical implications, and also because some scholars do not think that findings from a lab setting necessarily translate to natural settings. As such, this book does not provide an in-depth look at experimental design.

Mapping Empirical Writing Center Research

As a writing center researcher, you'll participate in a scholarly conversation that has been going on since the late 1970s and early 1980s.[3] It was in 1977 that Muriel (Mickey) Harris started *The Writing Lab Newsletter*, which began as an informal way for writing center directors to keep in touch and later became a **peer-reviewed** publication. Following closely behind, in 1981, the first issue of the *Writing Center Journal* premiered, and in 1982 the first meeting of the National Writing Center Association (later to become the International Writing Center Association) was held. As these venues for sharing scholarship and research on writing centers coalesced, the subfield began to take shape. For the remainder of this chapter, I want to outline in very broad (and necessarily crude) strokes a brief history of writing center empirical research to provide a starting point, especially for those new to this area of study. As you'll see, the history of writing center empirical research is intertwined with the history of Rhetoric and Composition research and (classroom) pedagogy.

The Process Movement

In Rhetoric and Composition, the 1970s and 1980s were the heyday of what is now called the process movement. During these decades, many instructors of writing moved from a focus on product—finished papers—to a focus on process. As a result, many composition instructors began to teach students how to brainstorm, draft, revise, and edit their work as part of the overt instruction in the course. In process-based classrooms, student grades were awarded for both completion of the process (e.g., multiple drafts and revisions) as well as on the final product. Donald Murray's 1972 article "Teach Writing as a Process Not Product" was a rallying cry for many instructors. Murray outlined the process as prewriting, writing, and rewriting, and he provided ten implications for how instruction would necessarily change if teachers focused on process. One key difference in the process movement over older models was the focus on prewriting. Older models of instruction might provide students with an argument to make, a format for the argument, and, sometimes, the evidence to support that argument. Murray and others suggested that the key component of good writing was having good ideas; as such, Murray suggested eighty-five percent of writing time should be given to prewriting in which students could come up with their own ideas and evidence.

A second concept that grew to greater prominence during this time was collaboration, especially peer collaboration. In older models of composition, lecture was the primary vehicle for delivering instruction; in the process movement, more and more teachers would devote class time to peer feedback. Writing scholars such as Peter Elbow and Kenneth Bruffee emphasized the value of peer feedback for both the writers, who could see how their writing was understood, and for readers, who could see how other students were exploring ideas in writing. In "Collaborative Learning and the 'Conversation of Mankind,'" Bruffee argued that our thinking was only as good as the conversations we have, therefore, writing classrooms need peer conversation to produce better student writing (421).

The sense that peers were essential for good thinking made the 1970s and 1980s a great boom period for writing centers, too—hundreds of writing centers opened during this period. The writing center idea was sold as a site that provoked prewriting and provided peer feedback; students could go to the writing center to brainstorm ideas and to be involved in conversations about their drafts. The most well-known passage from writing center scholarship came from this period and shows advocacy for process over product, too; Stephen North wrote, in "The Idea of a Writing Center," that

> [i]n a writing center the object is to make sure that writers, and not necessarily their texts, are what get changed by instruction. In axiom form it goes like this: Our job is to produce better writers, not better writing. Any given project-a class assignment, a law school application letter, an encyclopedia entry, a dissertation proposal—is for the writer the prime, often the exclusive concern. That particular text, its success or failure, is what brings them to talk to us in the first place. In the center, though, we look beyond or through that particular project, that particular text, and see it as an occasion for addressing our primary concern, the process by which it is produced. (438)

North's assertion, which follows others from the process movement, was that writing instruction should be more concerned with a writer's overall development and not on any single writing task; process, not product.

Along with the shift toward process in the teaching of college composition, Rhetoric and Composition empirical researchers began researching the writing process. One popular method for doing so was called the "talk-aloud protocol," in which the researcher would ask participants to write something and to say aloud every thought that he or she has while trying to write it (see Linda Flower and John Hayes for the most well-known example of the talk-aloud protocol). Doing so, these researchers were trying to make visible the invisible process of writing. Similarly, researchers compared different levels of writers to see if their processes were notably different (e.g., Nancy Sommers; Sondra Perl). The hope of these researchers was, again, to make visible different writing choices or goals of better writers to teach the process of more experienced writers to less experienced ones.

Writing center empirical research during this time period centered not on the writing process, but on the tutoring process guided by Stephen North who advised that "Writing center research must begin by addressing this single, rather broad question: *What happens in writing tutorials?*" ("Research," 29, emphasis added). North laments that as of the mid-1980s not a single published study shows what happens in a writing center tutorial. However, now thirty years later, lots of writing center research has tried to answer that question to understand the process—really to make visible—what happens in "good" sessions, so that tutors can be trained to do more of the good and less of the not-so-good. In fact, by 2008, Boquet and Lerner say that "much progress has been made" in answering North's question (28), and Babcock, et al.'s *A Synthesis of Qualitative Studies of Writing Center Tutoring,* a review of two decades of published qualitative writing center research, state that the studies in the book all focus on "what goes on in a tutoring session" (5). You'll find many examples of studies throughout this book that take on North's question originating in the process movement.

Post-Process Composition

In the late 1980s, however, Rhetoric and Composition took what's been called a "social turn"—a turn away from the narrow focus on the act of writing to a broader understanding of writing. The social turn, John Trimbur describes, as a turn toward "a post-process, post-cognitivist theory and pedagogy that represent literacy as an ideological arena and composing as a cultural activity by which writers position and reposition themselves in relation to their own and others' subjectivities, discourses, practices, and institutions" (109). The process movement, critics argued, located writing too narrowly in minds or in individuals. Instead, Rhetoric and Composition scholars asserted, writing is a situated act that is innately social, material, mediated, and contextual.

For example, though I might sit by myself to type these words, I am influenced by the sources I've read, my previous experiences, my mentors, conversations, my Twitter feed, and feedback I receive (and anticipate) from my writing group, from the editors of this book, and from readers; that is, others influence my work even though I am physically alone. Writers are influenced, contained, and enabled by working conditions and various motivations; my ability and willingness to write these words depends on a job that rewards publication, a computer that reliably starts and saves my work, and an electricity bill that has been paid. Further, my ability to write and be read is a privilege that comes with my university faculty membership and my degrees—both of which were not earned by virtue of my whiteness, heterosexuality, cis gender orientation, and my middle-class upbringing, but certainly were not complicated by those factors. Furthermore, the history of so-called "academic writing," the historical ways of writing in my specific disciplines, the genres I enact, the rhetorical moves I make, and the types of evidence I provide all press on my writing choices—directing, restricting, and organizing my thinking and writing. Thus the act of writing does not start or end when I am typing; the act of writing is entangled with many other people, histories, genres, places, objects, and factors.

The social turn then brought—to a larger degree than ever before—the consideration of race, gender, class, sexuality, privilege, genres, spaces, institutions, and technologies as substantial factors in writing, the teaching of writing, and the study of writing. When this happened, the word "post-process" began to surface as a term that signified both the movement that came after the process movement chronologically and, yet, also as a term that retains the lingering influence of the process movement, Process 2.0 if you will. Post-process pedagogies typically retain the belief of writing as a process and the necessity of others for feedback into that process.[4]

Second, the post-process movement shifted the focus away from pedagogy. In the Introduction to *Beyond Postprocess,* Sid Dobrin, J. A. Rice, and Michael Vastola assert that the resistance to the process movement was also resistance to the idea that there was one process that could be taught or learned by all writers for all writing situations. They see a possible trajectory of Rhetoric and Composition scholarship away from pedagogy and thus composition altogether. They write, "[W]e contend that any move beyond postprocess be understood as inherently postpedagogy—not opposed to composition studies' pedagogical imperative, but more interested in questions and theories of writing not trapped by disciplinary expectations of the pedagogical" (14). In other words, the authors suggest the field is widening its gaze to see all sorts of writing acts (certainly, as they note, including new media compositions) not just those composed by students for a particular class. Thus, researchers in Rhetoric and Composition are no longer only or primarily focused on studies that will show us how to teach (or tutor) better.

These two key components of the post-process movement—writing as a situated, mediated, social act and Rhetoric and Composition as moving post-pedagogy (or at least moving past codified universals in teaching and tutoring)—are evident now in the scholarship and empirical research of the field and in the subfield of writing center studies. Evidence of post-process values are apparent in most recent theoretical writing center scholarship (e.g., Geller, et al.; Grimm; Denny; Sheridan and Inman; Greenfield and Rowan; Condon). However, less writing center empirical research reflects the change from process to post-process. Writing center research needs to move toward research methods that better capture the situatedness of writing center work and toward studies that, in addition to studying the tutorial, also move beyond that narrow focus suggested by North some thirty years ago to explore other aspects of writing and writing center work.

For instance, Paula Gillespie, Brad Hughes, and Harvey Kail have been collecting data for years on "tutor alumni"—those students who used to work in writing centers—and their lives post-writing centers. The researchers use surveys and also focus group dinners to understand the benefit of writing center work for tutors—not to improve the act of tutoring, but to better conceptualize the multifaceted benefits of a writing center. This kind of empirical study is able to capture complexity and situatedness through its longitudinal, qualitative design; we need more studies in writing center studies like this one.

Throughout this book, I'll cite a number of writing center empirical research studies from across the decades, some of which are influenced by the process movement and some by the post-process movement. As key values of the process movement of invention and collaboration remain in the post-process movement, much of the process era scholarship is still of value today. However, a post-process consciousness is of value for emerging writing center scholars to remember:

- the act of writing as mediated, situated, political, and social;
- the act of tutoring as also mediated, situated, political, and social;
- the act of writing as irreducible to a single, step-by-step process;
- the act of tutoring as irreducible to a single, step-by-step process;
- the recognition of writing as more than simply text on a page;
- the work of writing center as more than tutoring; and
- the work of Rhetoric and Composition as more than developing a set of teaching practices for first-year college writers.

For Discussion, Reflection, and Action

1. Of theoretical, practitioner, or empirical, which type of research is most familiar to you as a scholar? How about as a research participant or subject? How about as a reader of research? Does this correspond to your academic background?

2. What practices in the writing center where you have worked seemed based in process pedagogy? What practices seem influenced by the post-process movement?

3. Brainstorm a list of potential topics for writing center research that focus on tutoring and then brainstorm topics that focus on other aspects of writing center work.

Recommended Resources

Dobrin, Sidney, J. A. Rice, and Michael Vastola, eds. *Beyond Postprocess*. Logan, UT: Utah State UP, 2011. Print.

Kent, Thomas, ed. *Post-Process Theory: Beyond the Writing-Process Paradigm*. Carbondale: Southern Illinois UP, 1999. Print.

Liggett, Sarah, Kerri Jordan, and Steve Price. "Mapping Knowledge-Making in Writing Center Research: A Taxonomy of Methodologies." *Writing Center Journal* 31.2 (2011): 50–88. PDF.

2 Getting Started

Readers of this book will be properly suspicious of presentations of cut and dried, linear, straightforward processes because we know that the writing process, for one, is often presented as simple but in practice is complex. The same is true for the research process. This chapter introduces you to the steps of an empirical research study. There are surely steps you should not omit; however, I won't suggest that the steps are a series of stages easily checked off in order. Like writing, researching is recursive; you'll return to different stages (even when you really don't want to!). Also like writing, you'll encounter new information and new obstacles along the way that will send you back to the start to refine your study. So, as I describe steps in a typical writing center research project, know that your project will take its own path and know that you may be working on several stages simultaneously. Research is messy, it's true. But the complexity of it is often what keeps researchers engaged; research calls for problem solving of the highest degree.

Second, this chapter walks you through the process of drafting a research proposal. Research proposals for empirical studies are often required for class or graduate projects, for grants, and for Institutional Review Boards (IRBs). Since writing center research projects often involve human participants or writing samples, the research proposal is a safeguard. You will need to convince others (your instructors, your committee members, your institution) that you have a solid plan for your research—grounded in current research practices and topics—and that your study will bring no harm to yourself, those who participate, or to your program or institution.

The Research Process

Writing center research is inquiry related to the work of writing centers broadly conceived. Writing center research might examine the places where writing center work happens, the people (attitudes, beliefs, and goals) involved in writing center work, the language or texts exchanged in writing center work, the tools or technologies used for writing center work, or the scholarship and pedagogy informing writing center work. As mentioned in the previous chapter, much writing center research has focused on the act of tutoring, yet newer theories ask us to also consider other dimensions and angles of writing center work. To start a research project, you'll need to begin by narrowing your focus to one particular aspect you'd like to study.

Identify a Research Problem

If you've decided to conduct a writing center research project, you'll first want to isolate a research problem. A research problem is more than a mere topic. I might decide I want to study something with technology in my writing center. That is a topic—a broad one, for sure. However, a **research problem** identifies a gap between *what we know* and *what we need to know*. Mary Sue MacNealy says that "good research projects often arise from some kind of dissonance, such as a clash in beliefs, a lack of important information in some area, or expectations that are violated in some way" (128). Let's consider an example. Suppose I notice by tracking analytics that our writing center blog readership is down over the past six months. That is something that I know, yet I might not know why. That gap could be my research problem.

However, there are many gaps in our knowledge and not all require a research study to remedy them. After isolating a research problem, ask yourself these questions:

1. Can I find the missing knowledge by consulting someone, from source materials, or from institutional data?

2. Do others recognize this information gap or do others believe they know the knowledge I'm lacking?

3. How important is it for me and for others that I acquire the missing knowledge?

4.   Is it knowable?

In my hypothetical case, I can't look for reasons for drop in readership of our writing center blog by looking at writing center scholarship. Though there are sources that speak about using blogs in writing centers, none will tell me what is happening in my local context. Likewise, there is no place I can go for data. If I talk with others on staff at the writing center, they may think they know why readership is dropping—they may provide reasons I find convincing enough to believe and no longer need to pursue the issue. If not, though, I can then weigh how important it is that I acquire the missing piece of knowledge. Will it make some significant difference to me, to people in my local setting, and people in my discipline if I pursue it further? In my case, I'm not sure it will. It may satisfy only my own curiosity, so that would limit any usefulness. However, in a different setting where I have received funding for my social media endeavors, a drop in readership would be important to understand. The right study could help me discern the reasons for the change in readership; it is knowable.

Asking yourself these questions about your research problem can help you discern whether your problem is really one worth researching. Many times my students and I have become fascinated with finding something out, but have had to come to terms with the reality that it is only a lack of knowledge that we alone are missing or that it doesn't really have any significance to others. There is no problem with satiating curiosity—you *can* investigate something that piques your interest—unless your research has other motivations. Say, for instance, you want to publish your findings or use the research for a graduate project that must contribute to the knowledge base of the field. You might not be able to publish or defend a project that is so idiosyncratic that it only interests you.

Look for Related Sources

Even though you are trying to answer a question that has, as of yet, no answer, doesn't mean that you can't find related, relevant sources on your topic that use your research methods to help you shape your study. Researchers consult sources (also called **secondary sources** or secondary material) often. Researchers want to see who else has written on a similar topic or have tried to address a similar research problem. You might find all types of scholarship on your topic (theoretical, practitioner, and empirical). Take note of what you find. What aspect of your topic has been studied already? In what type of approach? What hasn't?

In writing center studies, secondary sources can be found through several portals:

CompPile.org: This website hosts a massive database for Rhetoric and Composition. The journals that most frequently publish articles on writing center work are included here. I use this site as my first stop in starting a research project. The search function is persnickety (writing center texts are found with the keyword, w-center, for instance), but once you figure it out, you'll find this site indispensable.

wlnjournal.org: This is the digital home to one of the key peer-reviewed journals in the field, *WLN: A Journal of Writing Center Scholarship* (formerly, *The Writing Lab Newsletter*). This site archives all issues of the journal except for the current year. There is a search function, but it is rather rudimentary. It is easier to use CompPile for searching terms and wlnjournal.org to find the issue by year.

Writing Center Research Project (http://casebuilder.rhet.ualr.edu/wcrp/): This site archives issues of the *Writing Center Journal* up to 2005 and has some information on a the Writing Center Research Project surveys and oral histories.

JSTOR, Academic Search Premier, other library-subscription databases, or Google Scholar: If you are on a college campus, you'll likely have access to a variety of academic databases through your library. If you are unfamiliar how to use these databases, ask a reference librarian for help. If you don't have access to a college library, you can do a similar search via Google Scholar. When possible, Google Scholar will link results to full-texts of articles.

WorldCat, Amazon, or Google Books: If your library has access to WorldCat, you can search for topics among nearly every book in print. If not, Amazon.com or Google Books works pretty well for this purpose, too. You can then see if your library has a copy of the book. If not, you can request the book through interlibrary loan. Sometimes Amazon or Google Books has an online preview of the book available or a sample chapter available online or via a download to a Kindle or Kindle app (or similar e-book reading devices or apps).

A Synthesis of Qualitative Studies of Writing Center Tutoring 1983– 2006: This bibliographic book synthesizes qualitative research studies on tutoring by topic. Many of the included studies are theses and dissertations.

ProQuest Dissertation database: Many writing center studies are published as dissertations and not in other formats. Typically, the first chapter or two of a dissertation is available for free in this database; however, a researcher may have to pay for access to an entire dissertation if the researcher does not have a library who can borrow a dissertation by interlibrary loan.[5]

Many, many times when I've isolated a research problem, I'll consult sources, and I'll find an article that seems to do exactly what I'm trying to do. In the moment, this can be paralyzing and deflating. However, if I sit with it awhile, I can usually find the point where the previous research ends and where I can pick up. For instance, if the article uses theoretical inquiry, can I follow up with empirical inquiry? I've come to expect these moments and now know that finding sources that speak so directly to my research problem are tremendously helpful as a launching point; they clarify for me that the topic I'm interested in is interesting to others.

Occasionally, I'll have the opposite problem and not find much existing literature on the topic. For example, I wrote a technology column called "Geek in the Center" for a couple of years. In it, I would often consider available technologies for writing center work. Many times I would not find directly related sources because the technologies were new. In those cases, I had to broaden the scope of my search for secondary sources to include sources that were less directly connected—say research on newsletters in writing centers when discussing blogs.

Regardless, when you gather source material, read it closely and begin the work of summarizing what the works say individually and synthesize what they say all together. This summary and synthesis becomes the **literature review** in your proposal or research report. Many literature reviews take a deficit strategy; that is, the research points us to what *has* been studied and what *has not* been studied on a particular topic. Pointing to the deficit, the researcher tells us how his or her research will help fill that gap.

Though it is not always the case, many times what you want to study lies at the intersection of several areas, and it can help to draw out the overlapping ideas and the gap where your study lies. I often ask my students to plot out three intersecting circles (you might have more, of course) and name the circles according to the topics and/or methods converging in their project. For example, if I took on the study of blog readership, my plot might look like this:

Figure 1. Mapping a Niche

Scholarship that falls within any area on this Venn diagram might be appropriate to review for my study. Those articles and books that fall within a spot where two circles overlap are likely more important for study. Those that fall within the center triangle, where all three circles overlap, are very close to your project. Often, the center spot will have no sources because that is the gap in the research you are hoping to fill. If you find that the center spot has five, ten, or twenty relevant studies already, you need to zoom in more. You haven't yet identified a gap. Being able to see how closely related other studies are to your own is helpful in drafting a literature review, which is discussed more at the end of this chapter.

Cultivating a good working relationship with a colleague at your own institution or one nearby who has familiarity with Rhetoric and Composition and writing center studies research is crucial at this stage. You'll want someone who can help you decide if you need to zoom in or zoom out with your secondary source search. When you are a true newcomer to the field (as I was), it takes some time to understand what ideas have been written about by so many that they no longer press for attention. For instance, a project I did early on in graduate school was about prewriting—a topic at the time that seemed to me very important to the act of teaching and learning writing. When I submitted my project to a journal, the editor wrote a very kind reply explaining how the field was less interested in the idea of "prewriting" since more complex notions of post-process pedagogies had taken hold, and further, how the study I had designed to study prewriting had merits but I shouldn't generalize from my study (though I had). After this experience, I became better at seeking out professors and peers who could help me see the currency in my project and could point me to relevant secondary sources before I got too far along in my research.

Form a Research Question

Upon understanding what your study might add to the ongoing conversation, you'll want to draft a question that clearly articulates what you want to discover in your study; this is your **research question**. Research questions are notoriously tricky to write. Often the research question or questions are revised several times as the researcher clarifies his or her methods and goals. The key is making sure that you can answer your study with your methods and that the question you ask is the question you want to answer.

For example, in Laurel Raymond and Zarah Quinn's study of student goals, the research problem is that tutors have to negotiate student goals with their own tutor goals in a session (65). To focus their study, they formulate the following research questions:

• What writing concerns do writers bring to tutoring sessions?

- What writing concerns do tutors address?
- How do common writer concerns and common tutor concerns differ in distribution?
- When writers ask for help with a writing concern, to what extent does the tutor address this concern in the tutorial? That is, how often is the writer's specific concern fulfilled? Partially fulfilled? Not fulfilled? (65)

Notice that many of these questions are "what" questions. For qualitative research, the goal is often merely description. (In fact, qualitative studies are sometimes called *descriptive* or *narrative* studies for this reason; they describe or tell the story of an event, person, or place.) Yet, Raymond and Quinn's study is mixed-method, as their third question asks for a comparison of common writer and common tutor goals. This means counting to distinguish which goals are common for each and then making a comparison between the two groups. These questions clearly reveal to the reader what the researchers want to discover. Readers expect to see these research questions answered by the end of the study.[6]

Select Methods for Data Collection

As you work on reviewing existing literature and shape your research questions, you'll begin to think about how you can compile evidence that might answer your research question. Systematic ways of collecting evidence, or data, are called methods. There are many established methods for data collection and the bulk of this book—all of Part II—will walk you through some options, though other possibilities certainly exist. If you are new to research, you will need to familiarize yourself with available methods before you can cement a plan. Remember that planning for systematic data collection is one of the key components of the definition of research we are working under.

Think About Theoretical Frame for Interpretation

From the inception of your study, you should also be thinking about how you will read your data. How you make sense of data is called **interpretation**, and there are endless ways you could make sense of data. If you have a background in literature or the humanities, you know that scholars in these fields often read literature or historical events with a particular critical frame. A critical frame can be thought of as a pair of eyeglass frames; looking through the glasses I can see in a particular way. If I take those glasses off, I might see differently. For example, in Laurel Johnson Black's study, *Between Talk and Teaching,* she looks at how power manifests in teacher-student writing conferences. She uses a feminist critical frame, which means in shaping the study and analyzing the data, she paid attention to how gender and power played out in the conferences. Chapter 8 provides a more extended discussion of strategies for analysis and interpretation of your data, which could help you think ahead to how you will sort and read your data.

List Assets and Limitations

The most common issue I see in drafts of research plans by my students is ambition. Though I try to encourage big thinking, I often have to coach them to scale down the project to the size of, say, one dissertation instead of five. If we are lucky, we have many years to study writing center work. We don't have to study it all in the first study. So, it is important to take stock of what you have and what you don't have. For instance, I might have five hours a week I can devote to the study, but I might not have recording equipment or any funding. Jot down what you have available in terms of access, equipment, funding, time, collaborators, potential participants, and energy. Then, make note of what you don't have and don't have any way of obtaining or changing. Let these assets and limitations help you shape your study.

Obtain Permission and Consent

It is a mistake to get too far into planning a research project without thinking about where the study will take place, who will be the participants, or what data will be needed for the study. Any study conducted by any member of a college or university community that uses human subjects and will be publicly reported requires IRB approval. The IRB, or **Institutional Review Board**, is a group of people on every college campus that reviews research approvals to ensure that no harm will come to the participants in the study and to ensure that the benefits of the study outweigh the potential risks. If you are affiliated with one university and researching at another, you may need to obtain IRB approval at both schools. Likewise, if you have collaborators at different institutions, you will each likely need to apply at your own institution. Applying for IRB approval is different at each school, but you should expect to include the elements in the research proposal explained below. If your project isn't site-based, if it is a survey delivered electronically to tutors or directors across the globe for example, then it isn't necessary to obtain permission from the institutions involved or apply for IRB approval at each school, but it is still required that you get IRB approval at your own institution.

If you are researching at a college or university and plan to use the data to inform internal decisions or to present only to your class, to a writing center staff, or other university audiences, it may not be necessary to obtain IRB approval as there are exceptions for class-based research and for institutional research. When in doubt, ask. In my experience, I've been able to email the contact person for the IRB at my university, explain my project and what I'll do with the findings, and they've been able to direct me as to whether I need to apply or not.

Whether or not you need IRB approval, you will want to get permission and consent from those who supervise the site/program (if your project is site-based) and those who will participate. If you want to do an ethnographic study of a particular writing center, you will need to obtain permission from the administrator of that center. (Some IRB proposals require written and signed letters of permission from site directors in the application.) You will also want to make participants aware of what the study is for, what data will be collected, how the data will be used, stored, and reported. This information is typically contained in an **informed consent form** (see Appendix A for a sample). If you will take photos, video, or audio of your participants and will use those media in the reporting of the research, you will also want your participants to sign a **release form** giving you permission to do so (see Appendix B for a sample release form). Keep in mind that using a recording of your participants in the research report will compromise confidentiality; IRBs give increased scrutiny to these types of studies.

If you want to research at a K-12 writing center, you have other permissions you must seek. K-12 schools do not have IRB boards, but at some schools, principals or even school boards must vet all research projects. As the students will likely be under eighteen years old in these settings, you will also have to obtain parental consent to have students participate in the study.

Aside from permission, consent, and IRB approval, there are other ethical considerations you'll want to make right from the start of your study. You'll want to think about how your study might affect participants. Will your study affect their ability to do their job? Does it place an extra, uncompensated burden on them? Will potential participants feel obligated to participate (or to perform in the study in certain ways) because they know you or because you have a supervisory role over them? If your study reveals something potentially negative about a center, an administrator, a client, or a tutor, what will you do with the results? Asking yourself questions like these can help you design a study with care for the participants as a top priority.

RESEARCH PROPOSALS

As mentioned at the beginning of the chapter, a research project often requires a proposal for a class, a thesis or dissertation, or for IRB. The proposal is a pitch: you are trying to convince your readers that you have crafted a viable study on a topic that needs to be studied. Typically, a research proposal will contain the following:

1. An introduction which asserts the research problem and the research question(s). Often, but not always, in writing center studies an introduction starts with a narrative or personal anecdote which illustrates how the researcher came to be interested in the topic. Another approach is to begin with a summary of one or more secondary sources that leave off where you want to pick up.

2. A **review of relevant literature** (also known as a lit review). The review of literature grounds the reader. It asserts, "Here's what you need to know about my topic before you read what I'm going to do." Sometimes new researchers think that the audience they are writing to has already read everything in their lit review so they do not summarize or synthesize sources adequately. Don't make this assumption. Fellow readers of writing center scholarship will appreciate brief recaps of the sources pertinent to your study even if they have read the source before. Not every source, however, requires equal attention. Some sources that are tangentially related to your project may be referred to in a parenthetical only—sources noted in

the parentheses at the end of the sentence only. Sources that are closely related to yours in terms of topic, method, participants, and scope should be discussed at length—perhaps several paragraphs. Sources that fall in between these two extremes may be discussed in a couple sentences or a paragraph. Be sure that you arrange the discussion of secondary sources in a way that your reader can follow easily. Using subheadings is particularly helpful here; if you plotted out the areas of research that converge in your study, you could use these areas as your subheadings.

3. A **methods and methodology** section. If you are writing a proposal, it means that you are seeking approval to conduct your study. Perhaps the point of most scrutiny will be your methods and methodology section. Though the terms method and methodology are used in different ways by different authors, what you need to articulate is the overarching theory and assumptions guiding your study (or theoretical frame) which is your **methodology** and the tools or strategies you will use to collect data which are your **methods**. (Part II focuses on methods, so you will need to read on to make considerations of how you'll collect data.) Your methods section should be precise enough that someone else could pick it up and replicate your study. Importantly, a good methods section describes *how* you will conduct the study and *why*. Explain (using other sources as appropriate) why the plan you articulate is the best way to investigate your topic given your constraints.

4. Your reader will expect that you spell out the **population** under study if your study involves human subjects. The population is the entire group that you want to know more about—perhaps it is global, like writing tutors or writing center directors. Or, it might be local, such as first-year writers on your campus. In most cases, researcher cannot study an entire population, so they **sample** within the population. In brief, sampling means selecting certain people within the population to represent the whole population. (Sampling techniques will be discussed in more detail in discussions of surveying in Chapter 4.) Readers are also interested in knowing how you will **recruit** participants. This means explaining how you will entice (but not co-

erce) people within your population or sample to take part in your study. If you are using a set of texts, a **corpus**, you will need to spell out how you have gathered texts and which texts you'll study in your project and why.

5. Finally, your methods section should address reliability and validity. **Reliability** is the degree to which your study would yield the same results each time. (To remember this, think of a reliable car: one that gets you to your desired destination each trip.) In qualitative research, reliability is frequently established by having more than one person analyze the data. **Validity** is the degree to which a study actually studies the question at hand. (To remember validity, think about taking a train: to get to Istanbul, I have to have a valid ticket to Istanbul. A valid ticket to Helsinki won't do.) Qualitative researchers use **triangulation** (more than one data point) and **informant checks** to ensure validity.[7]

6. A **timeline**. Plot out how long you will take for data collection, analysis, and drafting your report. If this is your first research study, ask someone else who has more experience if your timeline seems realistic.

Once you have completed your proposal and gained approval to conduct your study, don't toss out the proposal. In many cases, the proposal is revised and becomes the first half of your research report—more on that in Chapter 9.

For Discussion, Reflection, and Action

1. Choose a topic related to writing center research and try out the various searches for related secondary sources listed in this chapter. Compare the results from the various searches.

2. Brainstorm a short list of research problems related to writing center work. Ask yourself the four questions about research problems to weigh the feasibility and practicality of pursuing any of the research problems on your list.

3. Find an empirical writing center research study (look ahead to Part II for suggestions if you need any) and see if you can

discern the research problem, research question, methodology, methods, population, sample (if appropriate), and recruiting strategies. Notice where in the research report these elements are discussed.

Recommended Resources

Blakeslee, Ann and Cathy Fleischer. *Becoming a Writing Researcher.* Mahwah, NJ: Erlbaum, 2007. Print.

Chiseri-Strater, Elizabeth and Bonnie Sunstein. *What Works? A Practical Guide for Teacher Research.* Portsmouth, NH: Heinemann, 2006. Print.

Cresswell, John. *Research Design.* 4th Ed. Thousand Oaks, CA: Sage, 2013. Print.

Nickoson, Lee and Mary P. Sheridan, eds. *Writing Studies Research in Practice.* Carbondale: Southern Illinois UP, 2012. 73–85. Print.

Research Notebook #1: Planning

Nikki Caswell, Rebecca Jackson, and
Jackie Grutsch McKinney

While drafting this book, I've been part of a collaborative writing center research project with two colleagues: Rebecca Jackson and Nikki Caswell. I've asked my colleagues to reflect with me on our project here to provide a glimpse into the sometimes messy but fascinating world of writing center research for those who are new to this area of inquiry. As a whole, Strategies for Writing Center Research *tries to lay out the process of research in a straightforward way, so the Research Notebook provides a necessary counterbalance to that; it reveals how the research path is twistier than planned. You'll find three parts to our Research Notebook—one included in each part of the book—so that you can see the challenges we faced at different stages in our research.*

A couple of years ago, Rebecca and Jackie conducted a national survey of writing center directors about the work—specifically the non-tutoring work—done in writing centers. It was our hunch that the work of writing centers was complex, but it was often unproblematically simplified as "tutoring." The survey confirmed our hunch and helped us complicate the idea that the work of a writing center was (just) tutoring (see Jackson and McKinney for more).

However, the most interesting bits of data collected in that survey never made it into the article or conference presentations where we reported on the data—yet the data stuck with us. The open-ended answers from the survey hinted at radically different ways of "being a writing center director" both materially and conceptually. We were intrigued with the small glimpse we got from the survey respondents and wondered, then, not just *What is the work of writing centers?* (as our first survey asked), but *What is the work of directing a writing center?*

On finding that little scholarship had been done on this topic specifically and no empirical research at all, we decided we should try to answer the question. We toyed with the idea of sending a second survey to query this, but we wanted to probe deeper than a survey allowed us. Both of us had used interviewing in past projects and felt that qualitative interviews would give us the rich, first-hand accounts we wanted. We quickly decided that we wanted to have a series of interviews with directors over time because, in our own experience, the work of directing a center evolves quickly. Given geographic, financial, and scheduling realities, we decided to limit our participants (6 directors) and length of time (one academic year).

The next question was who? Though the project could have proceeded in several directions, we decided to study new directors because their roles and work would not yet be normalized. That is, since the material and conceptual manifestations of their work had not yet fallen into familiar patterns, we imagined that they would be able to see it and render it visible to us. A long-time director, we feared, might instead unconsciously skip over any aspects of the work that they deemed "normal."

We started thinking of people we knew (mostly former students) who were starting in writing center positions. We informally asked a few people if they would be interested in participating in a year-long case study. One of those people was Nikki. Since Rebecca and Jackie were some years removed from our first writing center director positions, we realized it would be helpful to have someone on the research team who was in the midst of navigating his or her first year to help offset blind spots we might have. So, we asked Nikki to move from possible participant to co-researcher. She agreed.

Each of us had slightly different interests for the project; we did our best at this stage to make the study coherent yet open enough so we could each follow our own particular research interests. The next step was to clarify our research questions and to draft initial interview questions for our IRB proposals. We are all at different institutions and each required a different IRB application. It took over a month to draft, revise, and, finally, obtain permission from each of our separate institutions to proceed with our research. Though we had hoped to finalize approval before the academic year began, it just wasn't possible. This delayed our seeking participants and meant we didn't get interviews with directors before their job started, as we had originally hoped.

To diversify the cases, we sent a formal query to WCENTER (a mailing list of writing center professionals) and the high school writing center list for participants. We wanted new directors—at the start of their first or second year on the job. They had to agree to monthly interviews throughout the academic year. Luckily, we had about fifteen people respond with an interest in participating, in addition to the few participants we already knew. Though we had originally conceived of the project with six cases, we decided on nine participants after having such interesting people volunteer. We thanked all of the volunteers and sent informed consent forms to all nine participants. After they signed, we set up initial interviews.

We decided the easiest way to proceed was to divide the nine participants into three groups and to have each of us on the research team interview one group, monthly, throughout the academic year. That way the work would be evenly distributed and each interviewer could develop a relationship with her participants over the course of the year.

We also believed that the participants should get something from their participation. Many participants noted what they wanted out of participating, such as "good research karma," a time to reflect on their first years, or someone to document their work. We also offered to be a sounding board or a resource for the new directors; an offer inspired by Jessica Restaino's similar offer to her participants in *First Semester* that some of the participants accepted.

Thus, without a single physical meeting, no funding, and no special equipment, we began our collaborative longitudinal study of new writing center directors.

Part II

3 Studying Texts and Talk

One of the most common strategies for studying writing center work, particularly tutoring, is discourse analysis. **Discourse analysis** is the study of language in use—in written, gestural, or oral form. Contemporary discourse analysis is frequently conducted by linguists, but scholars from other domains also use it to understand something about language use and to speculate on what that language use might mean to the culture. As Barbara Johnstone explains, "Discourse analysts work outward from texts to an understanding of their contexts, trying to uncover the multiple reasons why the texts they study are the way they are and no other way" (27). Thus, studying writing center talk and texts can tell us something about the contexts in which they originate. Moreover, Thomas Huckin notes that "[s]ociolinguistic research has shown that communities are created and maintained largely by their language-using practices" (85). As such, studying the language-using practices of those involved in writing center work can tell us something about writing centers and the communities that interact within those sites.

WHY USE DISCOURSE ANALYSIS?

In "The Idea of a Writing Center," Stephen North says that study of the talk about writing that happens in writing centers is desperately needed. "If the writing center is ever to prove its worth in other than quantitative terms," he writes, " . . . it will have to do so by describing [tutorial] talk: what characterizes it, what effects it has, how it can be enhanced" (56). Though I don't think writing centers struggle "to prove their worth" as much now as when North wrote in the 1980s, discourse analysis can help writing centers describe concretely what is said in writing center tutorials and other writing center work, what is said in writing center generated materials, and what is said in writing center scholarship. Moreover, Sharon Meyers and Claire O'Leary (in separate articles) both suggest that understanding discourse analysis can help tutors improve their tutoring. That is, if tutors better understand how culture is represented and enacted through language use, tutors might become more conscientious language users.

Discourse analysis, as the study of "natural" language use, is appropriate for studying written, oral, and gestural language. It is not a method for understanding perceptions or seeking to discover personal experiences or histories, nor is it the ideal method for understanding how users use tools or for taking action. For discourse analysis, a researcher starts with collecting or curating a set of texts with a belief that how speakers and writers use language is interesting and important for what it might tell us about the relationships of the speakers and writers involved at both the interpersonal level and the cultural level.

For example, if I sense that tutors at my writing center approach graduate student writers differently than undergraduate student writers, I might use discourse analysis as a way to examine this difference. I might or might not find differences in the word choice, tone, gestures, hedging, questioning and so forth that occurs in recorded sessions. Let's imagine that I discover a pattern of tutors interrupting undergraduates but do not see the same pattern of interruption with graduate students. This finding might suggest something to me about the power dimensions in the tutoring sessions and might let me speculate about the tutor-graduate student relationship more broadly.

Types of Discourse Analysis

Guides to discourse analysis will categorize and arrange types of studies in a dizzying variety of ways. James Paul Gee, for one, suggests twenty-seven tools for conducting discourse analysis in *How to Do Discourse Analysis* (x). Here, I'll simply divide discourse analysis into two broad categories: conversational analysis and document analysis. Though certainly finer distinctions can be made, most existing writing center discourse analysis research falls into these two broad categories.

Conversational Analysis

Conversational analysis is the study of discourse exchanged between two or more individuals. Typically the discourse is verbal and recorded by the researcher. The researcher uses the recording to craft a **transcript**—a word by word written representation of the conversation. Some transcripts also include additional linguistic and contextual information, such as time elapsed between speakers, interruptions, laughter, gestures, and noises or activity happening near the conversation, such as an airplane flying overhead (more information on creating transcripts can be found in Appendix D). The point of conversational analysis according to Peter Mortensen is to "attempt to make sense of talk from the perspective of its participants" (106). Conversational analysts, Mortensen explains, "generally accept the basic tenet that people use conversation to negotiate the tacit rules that govern their actions in social settings" (106–7), and writing center studies using conversational analysis do try to uncover those tacit rules.

Several theories about language use help discourse analysts focus their research gaze and interpret their data. For example, Jane Melnick draws on speech act theory as a theoretical frame to pay attention to competing needs in her own tutoring sessions in her article "The Politics of Writing Conferences: Describing Authority Through Speech Act Theory." She writes, "I wanted to know not only what the words of both participants were saying but also what they were doing. Speech act theory, I began to realize, might help me tell when and how I took control of the conference, or how I turned it over to the student" (10). Thus, Melnick's analysis of tutoring sessions focused on power; speech act theory gave Melnick a way to see power enacted in the words of tutors and students.

Likewise, in *Between Talk and Teaching* Laurel Johnson Black studies the transcripts of teacher-student conferences. She, too, is interested in how power manifests in these conversations (which as the title suggests she sees conferences as a hybrid genre somewhere between "natural" conversation and classroom teaching). For instance, in her analysis she suggests that even something seemingly mundane as the teacher's use of the word "and" is meaningful (46). Teachers will use it to connect disparate ideas—to suggest coherence—and at the end of a phrase to maintain the floor (or **talk turn** as it is often called in discourse analysis). Black also teases out power differences as related to gender and cross-cultural conferences.

Alternatively, many writing center studies, and conversational analysis in general, focus on politeness and other conversational norms. These studies pay attention to violations of unspoken norms and consequences or misunderstandings that result. Susan Wolff Murphy, for one, uses Erving Goffman's theory of self-presentation and Penelope Brown and Stephan Levison's theory of politeness to read eight tutoring sessions. For example, in one session described in length by Murphy, she notices a tutor's repeated use of first person plural in talking to a student. The tutor was frustrated with the student who wanted to write an essay but hadn't yet read the book the essay was to be based on. Murphy then suggests that perhaps the tutor uses first person plural (we) "so as to implicate himself in that behavior, which builds rapport and reduces the face threat of the accusation" (Murphy 77). Thus, conversational analysis can allow researchers to speculate on how language choices might reveal speakers' complex and competing purposes and emotions. Robert Brown uses another of Goffman's ideas, footing, in his analysis of twelve tutoring sessions (74). Footing is the relationship between the speaker's words and identity. Brown identifies four different ways that tutors take the role of audience for their clients in his data and speculates how each of these enactments affect sessions.

Diana Calhoun Bell and Madeleine Youmans draw on Goffman and also on Paul Grice's ideas of the cooperative principle in their study of sixteen tutoring sessions with ESL students. They notice that "international students who do not speak English as their first language are likely to misunderstand the rhetorical construct [of feedback norms] or find it inappropriate because of cultural understandings about the function and purpose of praise as part of the genre of response" (33). Thus, in cross-cultural conversations, differing expectations for how a conversation about writing will play out can result in some awkwardness for both speakers who are relying on differing norms.

Susan Blau, John Hall, Jeff Davis, and Lauren Gravitz also study ESL sessions in their article, "Tutoring ESL Students: A Different Kind of Session." In their discourse analysis of dozens of tutoring transcripts, they find that tutors often play the role of cultural informant. Their close-up analysis of language use by tutors gives them a vantage point to see that the tutors in the study are neither purely directive nor

non-directive, but rather vacillate between being collaborative and di-
dactic within a single session (3).[8]

Some researchers look beyond the words in analyses of conversations. For example, Carol Severino considers eighteen extra-textual
features in what she calls a rhetorical analysis of tutoring sessions.
These features include the speakers' age, gender, ethnicity, status, and
how long the speakers have known one another (56). Severino notes
that not every feature seems to affect every session but that paying attention to features of the speakers can help with analysis of talk (61).
Claire O'Leary, an undergraduate researcher published in *Young Scholars in Writing,* also pays attention to extra-textual features in her analysis of tutoring sessions. In her case, O'Leary pays close attention to
how gender might affect speakers' language use.

As writing centers move toward post-process understandings of
writing center work, researchers will look to other discourse in addition the tutorial to study. For instance, researchers may look to staff
meetings, training, workshops, conversations among tutors or among
clients to see what else we can learn about writing center work.

Document Analysis

Whereas conversational analysis focuses on typically oral conversations or dialogues, document analysis focuses primarily on written
communication. Document analysis (also called textual analysis) can
be used to pay attention to language use and the content of all sorts
of "documents" used in writing centers: mission statements, websites,
promotional items, handbooks, handouts, videos, director/staff communication, email groups, blogs, annual reports, training materials,
posters, and more. Note that many of these texts communicate in multiple modes—they might use image, sound, graphic design, or animation to communicate. Contemporary document analysis works on the
assumptions that "text" is broadly understood as anything that can be
read and all elements of a document whether visual, aural, or textual
ought to be considered in analysis.[9]

Document analysis is the type of empirical research most closely
related to theoretical analysis (as discussed in Chapter 1). In both approaches, scholars read texts and make interpretations. Admittedly,
the line between the two approaches is sometimes blurry. However,
the key distinction of document analysis as a type of empirical re-

search is that there is a predetermined set of texts to study and a predetermined plan for analysis. In theoretical analysis, the scholar does not determine which texts will be studied in advance; instead, the scholar reads to find particularly interesting texts to explore and might decide upon a theory for analysis while finding texts for analysis.

In contrast, for document analysis a researcher would need to select a **corpus**—a set of texts to review—from the start. For example, I might decide to review writing center websites for presentations of histories of particular centers. To do so, I might decide to review all writing center websites listed in the Writing Center Directory hosted by St. Cloud University, but that would likely be too many. So I can decide how to limit sites. Maybe I look at only websites in my own state. Or maybe I look at sites I randomly pick. Or maybe I look at websites that have at least three pages. As part of my research plan, I decide on the criteria for my corpus before I begin analysis with full knowledge that the range in that set might vary, and that it might or might not contain what I'm looking for.

Though there has historically been less document analysis than conversational analysis in writing center studies, the analysis of published scholarship is frequently the subject of inquiry. Jim Bell, for one, published a review of scholarship published in the *Writing Lab Newsletter* between 1985 and 1988. In his review, he's interested in the subject of each article published within the stated timeframe. A similar study recently won the IWCA article award, Dana Lynn Driscoll and Sherry Wynn Perdue's "Theory, Lore, and More: An Analysis of RAD Research in the Writing Center Journal, 1980–2009." Driscoll and Perdue categorize the articles based on the type of inquiry each article uses.

Laurel Raymond and Zarah Quinn analyze session documents in their study "What a Writer Wants: Assessing Fulfillment of Student Goals in Writing Center Tutoring Sessions." They write, "As undergraduate peer tutors ourselves, we wondered how well sessions conducted by our fellow peer tutors honored writers' requests. The purpose of this study was to analyze the fulfillment of students' initial concerns in writing center peer tutorials. Furthermore, the study examines which concerns are most common among students when they come to the writing center and which concerns tutors most commonly focus on" (65). The researchers used records of the writer's initial concerns and the session summaries written by tutors to see what concerns the writers had and what concerns were ultimately addressed. This study is a particularly nice example of how existing documents—through what David Gray calls "unobtrusive measures"—can be used as data points (424). Participants in Raymond and Quinn's study did nothing they would not ordinarily do as part of their job, so the collection of data did not place any extra burden upon anyone. Gray suggests other documents—such as informal archives and collections, digital archives, organizational information, and community data—might be available for unobtrusive collection (428). Many writing centers house these sorts of informal archives.

I've done my own small-scale document analysis in a column in the *Writing Lab Newsletter* "Geek in the Center: Twitter." In that column I looked at the ways in which writing centers were using Twitter. I began by limiting the Twitter accounts I'd review by selecting the first 25 accounts in my Twitter search results matching "writing center." Then I categorized the types of posts within a certain timeframe from those accounts. I noticed that active writing center Twitter accounts mainly posted only on whether they were open or closed, shared links, or, more rarely, posted about occurrences happening within their own centers (8). This type of analysis helped me to encourage readers of the column to think about the messages they posted to Twitter and to imagine what else they might do.

PLANNING AND CONDUCTING DISCOURSE ANALYSIS

Like all of the methods that are discussed in Part II, your first step is to make certain that the method is appropriate for finding answers to the research question you have asked. If you are curious about specific language use and want to speculate on what that language use means, then discourse analysis is appropriate as a method.

Next, you need to collect "real life" examples of language in use that will relate to your research topic. Your research question might specify special populations, say, writing center directors, tutors, or LGBTQ students. In that case, you'll obviously need to recruit participants who fit those populations. Likewise, if your research question specifies a topic or genre, your examples must reflect those. For instance, if your research question asks *What types of questions do tutors ask one another at staff meetings?*, you'll need to recruit participants who are tutors at staff meetings. Or, if you're curious about how writing center websites describe the work of writing centers, you'll collect examples of websites and not of other documents. Though there is no perfect number of documents or conversations to collect, most studies cited in this chapter record at least ten tutorials. Several record more and report on a smaller subset.

Sometimes researchers need to revise their research question, topic, genre, or populations based on access. In writing center studies, most discourse analysis is conducted in the researcher's own institution or with publicly accessible documents, so traveling or recruiting participants over a distance is not typically a concern for discourse analysis.

The greater wildcard in discourse analysis is whether the language use you want to observe happens naturally. Thomas Huckin suggests discourse analysts start with an initial corpus to see if the language use they are curious about is present (90). So, you might initially record two writing center staff meetings to see if tutors are asking any questions of one another. If they are, then you might decide how many additional meetings you want to record to use as your "study corpus" (Huckin 92). One graduate student I worked with wanted to see how tutors used pronouns (especially "we") in tutoring sessions, but in her recordings she didn't find them using pronouns very much at all. The best you can do is to get permission to record in situations where you think the language usage you are looking for is most likely to occur. Even if you don't find what you initially set out to find, that in itself can be informative. And, after you have collected the conversations or documents, you might be able to ask another question of the data. Jo Mackiewicz and Isabelle Thompson have noted that the various features that writing center researchers have looked at in tutorial transcripts include interruptions, closed or open questions, echoing, qualifiers, directives, mitigation strategies, volubility, backchannels, overlaps, number of words, amount of time the student held the floor, questions the student asked, questions the student answered, topics raised, and diminutive hedges (41–42). Thus, there are many ways to look at corpus data: you can always adjust your focus or collect more texts.

Conversations for analysis are always recorded and transcribed. Because of this, you'll need to consider if you want video or audio recordings. If you are interested in gestures or any contextual visual information, you will want to video record conversations. Moreover, I'd strongly recommend video recording conversations with more than two participants because it gets increasingly more difficult with audio recording to discern who is talking the more participants you have involved.

Similarly, for document analysis consider what contextual information you might want to collect along with your documents. If you are interested in language use on writing center blogs, you'll want to consider what counts as the blog—will you look at posts and comments? Shared links? Facebook or Twitter posts about the blog? Do comments about the blog but posted on Facebook or Twitter count? Think carefully about what will be important in making sense of your data. It is perfectly appropriate to collect more data than you end up using, so I'd recommend including related documents initially and deciding after data collection if the additional information helps or hinders your analysis later.

When you have secured permission from participants and from sites to record conversations, you should make the recording as unobtrusive as possible while still obtaining a quality recording. An entire film crew hanging mics over a tutoring session isn't necessary or optimal, but holding an audio recorder fifteen feet away won't work either. The researcher's presence might be more intimidating to participants than equipment. For that reason, setting up a good quality audio recorder at the table with two individuals or a small video camera on a tripod that will record all interactions within the frame are possibilities; the researcher then could turn on the recording device and leave the room.

It is essential to check and double check equipment in your research site before recording. Notice whether your recording equipment quits after a certain mark (is the memory full at 30 minutes?), whether action is happening outside of the frame, or whether the background noise is too intense. You might need to use individual microphones for each participant if voices are difficult to hear in your practice recordings. Transcribing is tedious enough; you don't want to compound that process by collecting poor recordings.

LIMITATIONS AND ETHICAL CONSIDERATIONS

The main ethical consideration to make in conversational analysis is to obtain permission from participants to record their conversation.

Be clear about when the recording device is turned on and off, and be clear about how the recording will be used. The IRB at your institution will ask what you will do with the recordings. In most cases with conversational analysis, researchers record conversations, transcribe the conversations, and delete the recordings.

Document analysis can prove to be a gray area for institutional review boards because when we have documents as data, we don't necessarily have "human subjects" as defined by IRB. For example, several years ago when I did a study of instant messaging use in my writing center, I had a data log of all instant messages coming in and out of our writing center account that we collected for administrative reasons (i.e., tracking usage). When I wanted to use the logs for (public) research, I contacted my IRB. It took several email and phone exchanges to settle on the right course. In the end, I was asked to have a third party remove all usernames (since they could be traced to individuals) and then I could use the data without applying for IRB clearance; my IRB determined that without usernames the data did not involve "human subjects." Another IRB could decide differently, so it might be worthwhile to discuss your data with your IRB before doing your research.

The primary limitation of discourse analysis is that the sample size is typically, necessarily small. Thus, one should not make generalizations from findings. For instance, if I find that tutors ask one another leading questions in the eight staff meetings I record at my center, I cannot say that this pattern holds for every staff meeting at my center or at all staff meetings worldwide. Likewise, discourse analysts can state observed effects of a linguistic or rhetorical feature (especially if the effect is observable—e.g., someone laughs, nods, etc.), but they should be careful not to move too far into describing intent. We can't necessarily discern *why* a speaker used a particular phrase or linguistic feature from discourse analysis alone.

Summary of Key Points: Discourse Analysis

- Discourse analysis is the study of language in use: written, oral, or other.
- Oral recordings of speech are transcribed for study. Conversation analysis cannot be done well from just observation or listening to a recording.

- Discourse analysis can uncover tacit rules for language use. Many writing center studies use conversational analysis to understand the complex power dynamic in tutoring.
- Studies using discourse analysis may or may not need IRB approval, depending on whether or not there are "human subjects" involved (as defined by the IRB).

FOR DISCUSSION, REFLECTION, AND ACTION

1. What kinds of documents exist in your writing center, school, or university that could be used for a document analysis study of a writing center?

2. What patterns of language use do you notice in tutoring sessions at your writing center? Are there particular phrases you hear often in your writing center but rarely anywhere else?

3. Make a list of the anxieties you would feel if you were a tutor being recorded while tutoring. Then, make a similar list of anxieties you'd feel if you were a student being recorded in a tutoring session. Then, make a list of steps a researcher could take to alleviate as many of the listed anxieties as possible.

4. Most discourse analysis in writing center studies focuses on the tutoring session. What other conversations happen in or about writing centers? What could studying other non-tutoring conversations tell us about writing center work?

RECOMMENDED RESOURCES

Bazerman, Charles, and Paul Prior. *What Writing Does and How It Does It*. New York, NY: Routledge, 2004. Print.

Black, Laurel Johnson. *Between Talk and Teaching*. Logan, UT: Utah State UP, 1997. Print.

Gee, James Paul. *How to Do Discourse Analysis*. New York, NY: Routledge, 2010. Print.

Johnstone, Barbara. *Discourse Analysis*. 2nd ed. Malden, MA: Blackwell, 2002. Print.

Huckin, Thomas. "Context Sensitive Text Analysis." *Methods and Methodology in Composition Research*. Ed. Kirsch, Gesa and Patricia A. Sullivan. Carbondale: Southern Illinois UP, 1992. 84–104. Print.

Mortensen, Peter. "Analyzing Talk about Writing." *Methods and Methodology in Composition Research*. Kirsch and Sullivan. 105–29.

MacNealey, Mary Sue. *Strategies for Empirical Research in Writing*. Boston, MA: Longman, 1998. Print.

After the Study: *Laurel Raymond*

Laurel Raymond reflects on a collaborative research project with Zarah Quinn that started as an undergraduate class assignment and was eventually published in the Writing Center Journal *as "What a Writer Wants: Assessing Fulfillment of Student Goals in Writing Center Tutoring Sessions."*

Our study began as a final project for our peer tutoring class. At the outset, I think we had a naive idea that it would be simple; we just wanted to know if tutors really listened to writers' wishes. How hard could it be? It was the first empirical study either of us had ever attempted.

It quickly became clear that to answer our initial question, we had to ask and answer others—what does it mean to "listen" to a writer? How could we distinguish between writing concerns? What does "clarity" really mean? What about "flow"? It also became clear that answering these questions scientifically would take immense amounts of time, research, and refining.

Our original, "simple" idea was focused on our writing center alone. The numbers we provided were useful as a measure of our center's philosophy and success but are accordingly quite specific to our center. Looking back, I think that the enduring, generalizable value of our study thus lies not with our results, but with our methods, and with the supplemental questions that arose as a result of them.

As a result of the time we spent sifting through tutoring records, we realized that tutors and writers were using different terms for the same problems and the same terms for different problems. Even among trained tutors the language differed. Defining the ambiguous terms was our main challenge and one of our main contributions. It also underlies the study's main weakness: that we interpreted writers' wishes through the lens of the tutor's writing. Were we to revisit the study, we would correct this by including interviews and surveys with both the tutors and the writers in addition to the session records that we used.

The language ambiguity we uncovered and struggled with is also one of the more intriguing findings of the study, for it poses an important question: how do we as tutors know what writers are really asking for if the writers and the tutors are using different sets of terminology? Though this point is not emphasized in our original article, it is one we stress more heavily each time we present the study. As a result of the article, our writing center has continued its focus on writer-centered tutoring, but it has also started working with its writing instructors to provide writers with a more specific, standardized vocabulary to talk and think about their writing.

A valuable expansion of the study would be to look more closely at how writers and tutors use writing terminology, both in our center and in others, as well as to more closely examine sessions with goal-session mismatches. Teasing out the causes behind various mismatches could have implications for everything from the center's publicity to the overall shape of the university's writing program. In our writing center at least, our article sparked some of these changes, which may be, in the end, the result of which I am most proud.

4 Studying Individuals

Writing—and the teaching and tutoring of writing—is done by people, for people; writing center work is a human enterprise. Thus, many writing researchers are drawn to people as sources for answers to research questions. Writing researchers have asked questions such as: *What perceptions do individuals have about their writing or their teaching and tutoring of writing? How do they understand their work? How do they make decisions about their work? What kinds of writing do students, faculty, employees, or citizens do and why?* For many researchers, interviews play an integral role in finding answers to these questions.

Some researchers use interviews as the sole data point for a study, though many others use interviews in mixed-method approaches or with an activity theory, case study, ethnographic approach, or action research, (all of which will be discussed in later chapters). Regardless of the study design, learning to interview as a qualitative researcher is an important skill. Luckily for those who have experience working with students one-to-one in a writing center, interviewing requires some interpersonal skills that you may have already honed in tutoring. This chapter explores interviewing as a key method for writing center studies, pointing out along the way how those with tutoring experience can translate their skills to the task of qualitative interviewing.

Most people are familiar with interviewing because it is also used by journalists in print and digital media. However, because of the proliferation and the commonality of interviews—can we go a day without hearing or watching an interview?—some misperceptions might exist. For one, many conflate a journalistic interview approach and a qualitative approach. Though there is indeed enough overlap in these speech acts for both to be rightly called "interviews," journalists often interview to get a response to an issue (a source to quote) or a concrete answer (e.g., confirmation of a fact). Qualitative interviewers, however, are after something more. Irvin Seidman says that "the purpose of in-depth interviewing is not to get answers to questions, nor to test hypotheses, and not to 'evaluate' as the term is normally used. At the root of in-depth interviewing is an interest in understanding the experience of other people and the meaning they make of that experience" (3). Many qualitative researchers approach interviewing as a way to gauge how people make sense of their worlds. Importantly, Sharlene Nagy Hesse-Biber and Patricia Leavy note that interviews are a way to get at subjugated voices and knowledge (123); that is, we can interview to learn more about the experience of others underrepresented in existing research. Qualitative interviews let us dive deep with participants, to talk to them long enough that we walk away with a sense of their experiences and perspectives on those experiences. In brief, a journalistic approach to an interview seeks the "truth" and "facts;" a qualitative approach seeks perspectives and personal stories.

Another popular misconception of interviewing is that it is just like having a conversation. This seems logical if we consider a tutoring session a conversation, too. In a way, each involves speech partners taking turns talking to one another, but interviewing and tutoring have different norms and expectations than "normal" conversation. Interviews are typically recorded, transcribed, and studied through conversation analysis. However, researchers using interviews carefully select participants, schedule a time to meet, and plan questions or topics for discussion. As Kathy Charmaz notes in *Constructing Grounded Theory*, this process, violates conversational norms. She writes, "Although the intensive interview may be conversational, it follows a different etiquette. The researcher should express interest and want to know more. What might be rude to ask or be glossed over in friendly agreement in ordinary conversation—even with intimates—becomes grist for exploration" (26). The interviewer, as Charmaz notes, has a prescribed role in the interviewing situation and so does the interviewee. The interviewee constructs a narrative, a story for the interviewer (see Mould 90). Interviewees, perhaps more consciously than in ordinary conversation, try to package answers in a way that is intelligible and, perhaps, pleasing to the interviewers.

The misconceptions that the point of a research interview is to get "facts" or is simply to have a conversation leads some new researchers into jumping into an interview project without doing enough groundwork and preparation. Though there is much to interviewing that is relatively straightforward, qualitative research planning requires that we think through many decisions about a research method before beginning, such as whether interviewing is an appropriate method for our research topic and question, what type of interviews to conduct, how to formulate questions and conduct interviews, and how to collect the data of interviews.

WHY INTERVIEW?

There are many reasons that researchers turn to interviews to collect data. Here are just a few reasons given by qualitative researchers:

- Herbert Rubin and Irene Rubin: if you need complex answers, examples, or need to ask follow-up questions; if you want to understand how and why things change (2–3)
- Irvin Seidman: because you are "interested in other people's stories" (1)
- Robert Stake: to obtain unique information and interpretations; to find out about something that cannot be observed (95)
- David Gray: to examine feelings or attitudes (370)
- Charlene Nagy Hesse-Biber and Patricia Leavy: because "individuals have unique and important knowledge about the social world that is ascertainable through verbal communication" (119).

Similar reasons exist for writing center studies that use interviews. For example, Terese Thonus uses interviews as one data point in her dissertation study and subsequent article, "Triangulation in the Writing Center: Tutor, Tutee, and Instructor Perceptions of the Tutor's Role." Interviews were conducted and analyzed along with recordings of tutorials, assignment sheets and drafts, and tutor notes about tutorials. Thonus finds that interviews were key for determining how faculty conceived of tutor roles (63). In another study, Helen Snively, Traci Freeman, and Cheryl Prentice used interviews to ascertain local student needs (158). Additionally, Phillips conducts a three-part study to investigate support for multilingual graduate writers both locally and nationally. Interviews with seven graduate student "regulars" were able to flesh out trends noted in a survey. Thus, interviews can sometimes answer research questions that other methods cannot.

Types of Interviews

Many types of interviewing models are available for researchers to utilize. Researchers will want to return to their research question, their theoretical frame, and consider practical constraints when deciding which model to use. Oftentimes, interview types are categorized by the formality of the interviewing process, ranging from unstructured/spontaneous interviews on the one end in which the interviewer might think of a few topics to discuss or might just ask a few questions on the fly during ongoing fieldwork, to formal, very structured interviews where the interviewer asks the same set of interview questions to each participant in the same order and manner, almost as if doing an oral questionnaire. For example, Bojana Petric's *Writing Center Journal* article "Students' Attitudes Towards Writing and the Development of Academic Writing Skills," details a study that relied on a structured interview approach for data collection. Petric explains: "Interviewees were given a set of 90 prompts, in the form of written statements expressing an attitude or an assertion about a writing strategy, and were asked to respond orally, elaborating on their agreement/disagreement where they felt relevant" (12). Though highly structured, Petric notes that the interviewees would ask follow-up questions "about issues that seemed particularly important;" however, this must not have happened too frequently since interviews lasted only twenty to forty-five minutes (12). Falling in the middle of this continuum is a "semi-structured" approach in which the researcher develops questions or topics but deviates from the list and order based on desire to seek clarification and follow interests (for more, see Ann Blakeslee and Cathy Fleischer).

Yet other distinctions can be made about interviewing types based on goals, approach, and methods.

Topical Interviews

Topical interviews try to find the "facts" on a topic. This approach is used when a researcher is looking for a "a particular piece of information" (Rubin and Rubin 11). As such, topical interviews are related to journalistic inquiry where the focus is not on the interviewee's interpretations of his or her experiences. Herbert Rubin and Irene Rubin state that "the goal of topical interviews is to work out a coherent explanation by piecing together what different people have said, while recognizing that each person might have his or her own construction of events" (11). The researcher then acts as "more like a skilled painter than a photographer" by creating an account of what happened from the various answers (11).

In "The Seldom Heard Voices in Mary Lyon Basement: An Interview with Three College Writing Center Consultants," Alys Culhane takes a topical approach to interviewing; she selects three writing consultants based on a convenience sample and asks them each similar questions to "provide readers with a better overall sense of what consultants do, how they're trained, how they themselves put theory into practice" (87). Though Culhane does not take the painter approach suggested by Rubin and Rubin in reporting her findings. Instead, she reports on the interviews in a script-like fashion, writing the question she asked and then the interviewees' answers. There is no interpretation of the interviews (or at least obvious interpretation—she may have omitted or altered participants' answers); it isn't seen as data to analyze, but rather as "informational" (87).

Perhaps more closely aligned to the topical approach as defined by Rubin and Rubin is Birgetta Ramsey in "Re-seeing the Writing Center's Position of Service." In this project, Ramsey wants to find out what happened with the development of writing centers and writing programs in Sweden. She pieces together a narrative of the beginning of a Swedish writing center from various interviews (and observations) and does paint a picture of this recent event.

Spontaneous Interviews

Spontaneous interviews will occur during the course of participant observation (see more on participant observation in Chapter 6). The researcher will be among the people studied and may have the opportunity to ask a few questions. These opportunities cannot be sched-

uled, but they can be anticipated. Researchers in the field can stay alert
to moments when asking questions might be possible and appropriate.
Researchers won't typically pull out a recording device or a computer
to take notes because the opportunity for spontaneous interviews is
fleeting; however, Ann Blakeslee and Cathy Fleischer suggest having
this equipment ready if the setting allows for it (132). If not, you will
want to write what you remember of the discussion as soon as possible.
Spend time writing what you said and what your participant said, as
well as noting what the setting and context for the discussion was. It
will be particularly important in spontaneous interviews to do an informant check (more on this later in this chapter) to confirm that the
participant feels that you have recreated the scene well. Finally, keep
in mind that if you want to seize on these opportunities, you would
need to write this into your IRB proposal and your informed consent
forms at the start of the study; otherwise, you do not have permission
to use the interview data.

In-Depth Phenomenological Interviews

A specific type of semi-structured interview used frequently in qualitative research is the in-depth phenomenological interview. As the name
suggests, this type of interview aims to dive deep (thus "in-depth")
into the subject at hand and tries to listen for and report on the interviewee's perspective ("phenomenological"). Seidman describes the in-
depth phenomenological three-part interview series, based on the work
of Schuman and Dolbeare, in *Interviewing as Qualitative Research*. He
recommends that each interview last about ninety minutes and be
spaced three to seven days apart (14).

The first interview should be a focused life history. Here, "the interviewer's task is to put the participant's experience in context by asking him or her to tell as much as possible about him or herself in light
of the topic up to the present time" (Seidman 11). Seidman suggests
interviewers avoid asking *why* someone got to where they are and instead ask *how* (11). "By asking 'how?' we hope to have them recon-
struct a range of constitutive events in their past family, school, and
work experience that place their participation in [the topic at hand] in
the context of their lives" (11). So, a life history interview with a writing tutor might ask: How did you become a writing tutor? This question urges the tutor to consider what events and moments in their life

helped determine her fate. Asking "why" the tutor took up tutoring, she might instead list reasons for needing a job.

The second interview focuses on the details of his or her experience. In this interview, the interviewer concentrates questions on the concrete details. One way to do this is to ask for the interviewer to walk the interviewee through a typical day or week. Though the topic of such an interview for a writing center researcher might be "tutoring," it might be appropriate to have the interviewee talk you through a day, starting at the alarm clock and ending at lights out, so that you can get a better sense of how tutoring (or whatever the topic might be) fits into the person's life, rather than just asking the interviewee to discuss only "on the clock" hours.

The final interview in the three-part series asks that the interviewee reflect on the meaning of the activity/topic at hand. Seidman suggests questions that prod interviewees to reflect and interpret their engagement in the topic at hand and their lives. For example, he suggests asking mentor teachers a question like this: "Given what you have said about your life before you became a mentor teacher and given what you have said about your work now, how do you understand mentoring in your life now?" (12).

Active Interviews

As explained in James Holstein and Jaber Gubrium's *The Active Interview,* an active interview is less about what is asked and more about how the interviewer positions him or herself in relationship to the interviewee's answers. Thus, an active approach can be combined with other approaches in this section. Holstein and Gubrium critique the traditional view of interviewing, which they call the "vessel of answers" view, with an alternative they call the "activated subject" view (8). In traditional approaches, they explain, "subjects are basically conceived as passive vessels of answers for experiential questions put to respondents by interviewers. They are repositories of facts and related details of experience" (7–8). Instead, in Holstein and Gubrium's active approach, interviewers "invest the subject with a substantial repertoire of interpretive methods and stock of experiential materials. The active view eschews the image of the vessel waiting to be tapped in favor of the notion that the subject's interpretive capabilities must be activated, stimulated, and cultivated" (17). A traditional view imagines that an interviewee "serves up authentic reports" (8), and it is the job of the interviewer to interpret these reports. In an active interview, the interviewers understand that "all participants in an interview are inevitably implicated in making meaning" (18). That is, interviewees do not give neutral, or in Holstein and Gubrium's term "uncontaminated" interviews. As participants in the interview, they consciously select words, stories, and answers to provide while simultaneously not selecting other words, stories, and answers. Active interviewers keep this in mind and, as such, also ask interviewees to play a role in telling them what is significant from their perspective and what patterns emerge in their answers. In conventional interviewing, interviewers do this themselves in coding (more on this in Chapter 8), but the active approach shares interpretation with the interviewee during the interview itself.

So, let's say you are interviewing a community member about how she went from being a client of a community writing center to working there. A few times in the course of the interview, she mentions her neighborhood gardening group. Although initially you think that she's gone off topic and do not follow up on the gardening group comments, you eventually stop and ask: What connections do you see between your gardening group and the community writing center? This "active interview" type question, where during the course of the interview you ask about significance/meaning, could lead you to richer understanding and thus representation of the lived experiences of your participants.

Stimulated Recall

In "The Politics of Tutoring: Feminism Within the Patriarchy," Meg Woolbright reports on a case study project involving eight conferences between the same tutor and same student that she observes and records over the course of a semester: "My reason for doing this, and for conducting post-conference interviews with the tutor, was not only to learn more about what it is we do when we talk to students about their writing, but also to see if what tutors think they do when they tutor bears any resemblance to my interpretation" (18). The interviews in this instance are stimulated recall—Woolbright ask the tutor what was happening at certain points in the tutorial. For example, in one moment in the article Woolbright is following up on a part of the session where the tutor seems to be pushing the student to follow a certain path.

Woolbright notes, "When asked about this exchange, the tutor comes to a realization. She says, 'I just wrote the paper for her. I put it together. I didn't get her to put it together. And that's where things break down. She doesn't know what I'm talking about.' . . . [I]t is not until the tutor hears herself on tape that she realizes what she is doing" (25).

Thus, the benefit of stimulated recall—which can include bringing recordings, video, photographs, written documents or other artifacts to the interview—is in the ability of the artifact to stimulate a response in the interviewee. Perhaps, as in Woolbright's study, the interviewee might come to an insight prompted by the artifact that he or she would not have come to without the prompting. Stimulated recall interviews are helpful in writing center studies, like Woolbright's, where the interviewer wants to ask questions about a particular tutoring session. Without playing parts of the interview or sharing the transcripts, it might be very difficult for the participant to remember specifics. Likewise, a policy sheet, a screen capture, a class paper, a calendar page, or so forth, might help jog the memory of a participant in a non-tutoring study.

Focus Groups

Most interview studies assume one interviewer and one interviewee at a time, but there are other arrangements possible. One option for interviewing more than one person at a time is a focus group interview. Borrowing from marketing, focus groups are increasingly popular in qualitative research to hear from multiple participants efficiently. Having multiple participants at once can be attractive to possible interviewees who are hesitant to meet one-to-one with a researcher and, furthermore, the participants themselves can help stimulate memories of shared events. Gabrielle Griffin recommends focus groups with three to six participants that run for about ninety to one hundred twenty minutes (72). Often, food is offered as an incentive to participation, and the interview is led by a neutral party and recorded.

In *Noise from the Writing Center*, Beth Boquet describes using student focus groups in assessing her writing center (44). Notably, Paula Gillespie, Brad Hughes, and Harvey Kail also made use of focus groups in their well-known study of peer tutoring alumni. The team notes how focus groups preceded the larger (and ongoing) survey project, providing them with a "preview of some of the responses we would get in the survey, and the tutors in conversation with one another sparked lines of response a questionnaire alone wouldn't have produced" ("Focus Groups"). The team met for two hours with former peer tutors, over dinner, asking about eight questions/hour.[10]

Oral History

Oral history interviews are a type of historical research with living participants meant to both amend and preserve history. (Whereas oral histories are typically focused on an event or time period, life story interviews are similar but focus on a participant's entire life.) Since accounts of history tend to be univocal, accounts from those who have lived experience can create a fuller picture, a point that Carey Smitherman makes in "Conducting an Oral History of Your Own Writing Center." In this article, she discusses the Writing Center Research Project's aim to record, transcribe, and preserve oral histories of writing center leaders from the 1960s to the 1990s. For Smitherman, oral histories provide "a more personal approach to history" and "will serve the writing center community with a more accurate knowledge of its history" (2). Smitherman's article invites others to record oral history interviews to preserve writing center history.

PLANNING AND CONDUCTING INTERVIEWS

In most cases, careful preparations for interviews will be essential. This section provides some guidance in how to plan and conduct interviews for your qualitative research study.

Read Up

As discussed in Chapter 2, if you imagine that your study will contribute to an ongoing conversation, you should be aware of what is being said (and not said) in that conversation. Reading up on your topic may reveal that interviewing is or is not the best method for your questions, so it is a good idea to begin with this step. Whatever type of interview you select, you will need to do some advance planning to get the most out of your limited interview time. Begin by reading secondary texts on your interview topic and, perhaps, more on the specific type of interview you select (a list of recommended texts is provided at the end of this chapter). Furthermore, you may be able to read up on nonscholarly texts related to your topic, research site, or population. If you wanted to study the role of writing within student organizations on campus, for instance, you could research student organizations by visiting websites, social media sites, campus news archives, or find brochures in the student center.

Seek Participants and Schedule Interviews

Recruiting participants, as discussed in Chapter 2, can be difficult. Interviews require the gift of someone's time and demand a certain vulnerability. Most interviews do not rely on random sampling or make claims of generalizability. Instead, many qualitative interview studies rely on purposeful sampling (Seidman 45). There is no magic number for how many interviews you will need to do. However, David Gray suggests that about eight participants might be sufficient (376), and that number holds true for several writing center interview studies (see Phillips; Griswold, for example). Another way to decide on how many participants might be to follow Seidman's two criteria (48). First is *sufficiency:* are there enough participants to reflect the population? Second is *saturation:* you may have enough participants when you begin to hear the same/similar information reported. "The job of an in-depth interviewer is to go to such depth in the interviews that surface considerations of representativeness and generalizability are replaced by a compelling evocation of an individual's experience" (44).

The most obvious quality for participants is that they must have firsthand knowledge about your topic and be able to answer your questions substantively. Mould says to never pay participants for interviews (84), while Seidman says to be wary of participants who are too eager or too reluctant (47). Though it might seem easiest to start with people you know, Seidman warns, "My experience is that the easier the access, the more complicated the interview" (Seidman 34). People who know you might not take the interview as serious as others, might try too hard to give you answers they believe you might want, or might be hesitant to discuss their work with others that you might know, too. Though it is tricky to interview people you know, you still may if that is your only option given material constraints or given your topic. You can also ask people you know to recommend others. Difficult cases— ones that often draw more scrutiny from IRBs—involve interviewing people that you supervise, your own students, your acquaintances or friends (Seidman 35–36). Additionally, interviews with children under the age of eighteen require parental permission.

It is recommended to send a participant query to each possible participant directly (not a mass email) which gives the overview of your project, states a date range in which you hope to conduct interviews, notes where the interviews will take place and whether you will video/audio record the interviews, and estimates how long the interview will last. You will find you will get the best response if you are professional, courteous, and amenable. Consider meeting somewhere convenient to your participant (so long as the noise level is low). Interviews by email, Skype, or phone are options as well. Suggest several dates and times for the interviews.

Often researchers do not want to take up too much of a participant's time, so they make the interview as brief as possible. Though this instinct is a good one, researchers must safeguard from making the interviews so short that the resulting report suffers from reliability. I've been interviewed several times for student projects; on occasion, the interview was over in ten minutes. I'm not sure someone can fairly speak to my attitudes, beliefs, perspectives, and experiences after only ten minutes with me (though I do talk fast!). Hesse-Biber and Leavy recommend that interviews last one to two hours (124). Likewise, Seidman recommends ninety minute in-depth phenomenological interviews (17) and Griffin suggests ninety- to one-hundred-twenty-minute focus groups. For the interview project described in the Research Notebook in this book, our interviews were briefer than this typically, ranging from twenty minutes to just over an hour. However, our study was longitudinal, so we were able to accrue hours of interview time with each subject over the course of the academic year.

Draft Questions

Perhaps the trickiest part of interviewing is drafting questions that get you the answers you want without leading the participants to particular answers. Generally, open-ended questions will work better than closed-ended ones that only allow for a brief response. In their research guide for writing teachers, Elizabeth Chiseri-Strater and Bonnie Sunstein recommend questions like these to get participants talking:

- Tell me about a time when . . .
- What stands out for you when you remember . . . ?

- What's a typical day like for you?
- Tell me about the person who taught you to . . .
- Describe the story behind this. (125)

Above all, as Wendy Bishop writes, it is important to "check your wording for bias, infelicities, potentially insulting language, and predetermination. Don't try to get the answers you want or predict; allow the informant to inform you" (*Ethnographic*, 101). Mary Sue MacNealy suggests giving extra scrutiny to your first questions; do not, she advises, start with threatening or overly personal questions (204).

You won't need dozens of questions. Stake suggests planning just eight questions for an hour-long interview (97). Likewise, Bishop says you'll want four to twelve questions for a thirty to sixty minute interview (*Ethnographic*, 100). In Griswold's interview study of attitudes and knowledge of writing tutors, he asked nine questions and reported interviews often lasting more than an hour (71). In my own experience interviewing, I've learned that different participants have different response styles—some longer and some shorter—and will find different questions more provocative. One participant might utter a single sentence about a question and the next will talk for over ten minutes. That said, after drafting questions, it is a great idea to try them out on someone. The response can help you discern where revisions are needed. Some participants might want to see your questions before the interview to begin thinking about them beforehand. Oblige them.

Test Equipment

Rarely, a qualitative researcher would do an interview without a recording device. Recording an interview allows the researcher to return again and again to the actual words and phrasing of both the interviewer and interviewee and allows the researcher to create a **transcript** (more on transcripts in Appendix D). Some participants might not wish to be recorded—some may reject video recording but not audio recording. It is possible to work with participants or sites which do not allow recording by carefully taking notes and arranging for **informant checks**. Informant checks are when you ask participants to read and respond to your report for accuracy and veracity.

Most interviewers have anxiety about recording failures, and I think that anxiety is well-placed. I don't know a researcher who hasn't faced a recording obstacle. In the collaborative interview project discussed in the Research Notebook, we suffered a few recording losses. There was the interview we forgot to record. There was the interview we conducted with a different computer that we didn't test before beginning the interviews. There was the audio recorder that went missing for a few weeks in an office move. Sound quality wasn't an issue we had with this project but can be one that plagues the interviewer. Mistakes and failures happen. Check your equipment before the interview and check the recording directly after the interview. If something went awry, the interview will be fresh enough in your mind for you to write more notes, you'll know what changes you need to make before the next recording.

Conduct the Interview

When the day arrives for your interview, remember to get to your interview appointment early. Gray suggests arranging the seating so that the interviewee can't see your notes, not because you'll write negative comments or private thoughts, but simply because humans are curious and will be distracted by the notes if they can see them (379). Introduce yourself and the study even if you described it in a recruitment email. Check for understanding and ask for the participant to sign your **informed consent** form (see a sample in Appendix A). Start recording.

Ask your questions. Unless you are following a structured approach, there is no reason why you cannot opt to ask your questions in any order that makes sense to you and to follow up as desired, going off the script. Your key job during the interview is to listen and to perform listening. As Gray notes, "Where in normal conversation it might be acceptable to occasionally glance at one's watch or look away, in interviews a far greater degree of attentiveness is required" (383). Concentrate on what the interviewee is saying and take notes (these will be good to have in case your recording fails). You'll be listening to what the interviewee says and how she says it. You may naturally provide **back channel cues** (e.g., um-hms, yes, etc.), but you will want to be aware if you inadvertently lead participants with these cues (Seidman 74). If you have experience tutoring in a writing center setting, you probably have quite a bit of practice at listening closely, attentively, and paying attention to tone, time, and body language. You likely also have practice at allowing writers to lead. These skills are very similar to the listening skills you need for interviewing.

When an answer is given, consider whether you want to ask more about what is said or if you are ready to move on to the next question. Rubin and Rubin suggest that interviewers ask follow-ups to ask about perceived/actual gaps and omissions in answers and when interviewers can't understand the meaning of a response (13). The follow-up might be a **probe**, such as "Oh, can you give me an example of that?" which asks the interviewee to continue on with their current response. Interviewers, like tutors, also look for **markers**. Hesse-Biber and Leavy define markers as "important pieces of information that a respondent may offer as they are talking about something else" (129). A word, person, or event might be alluded to in one response that an interviewer returns to later after the question at hand is answered. It is nice to end the interview by asking the interviewee if there is anything else they'd like to say on the topic, if there is anything they had thought you might ask about. Oftentimes the answer is no, but sometimes they will have something to say or want to amend an answer given earlier in the interview.

Be aware of the time and do not go beyond the time frame you established at the onset unless the interviewee requests that you do. Be sure to thank your participant at the end of the interview and with a follow up email or note. Before leaving the interview, explain the next steps with your participant, especially if you want to share transcripts with the interviewee.

LIMITATIONS AND ETHICAL CONSIDERATIONS

It can be tempting to believe that you have a "representative" sample of participants and that what you find true is either generalizable for the general population or for a certain demographic. Resist this temptation. Your interviews—especially if you heed the advice to conduct long or multiple interviews and you allow for feedback on your transcripts/reporting—will contribute to the knowledge base surrounding your topic even though you won't be able to say that what you find is universal. Like many other methods for qualitative research, interview studies can paint a detailed portrait of individual attitudes, beliefs, experiences, and perspectives. That is what makes interviews rich, exciting, rigorous, and even, occasionally, moving.

As obvious as it sounds, the most important ethical safeguard you can make in an interview study is to be clear with your participants about the interview and what you'll do with the recording and notes you collect. This should be communicated at the point of recruitment, in the informed consent, and again at the end of the interview when you explain your next steps. As in any study, participants are able to leave the study when they wish. With interviews, I also make sure to allow participants to strike any language or any section of an interview in their review of the transcripts. In one case, this meant the participant wanted me to cut a portion that I felt was very compelling, but I obliged since I would want the same treatment as a participant in a research study.

SUMMARY OF KEY POINTS: INTERVIEWING

- Interviewing allows researchers to talk directly to the source and provides flexibility that surveys do not.
- There are many types of interviews. Qualitative research interviews typically try to understand the world from the perspective of the interviewee.
- Being clear with interviewees about how the interview notes and recordings will be used is essential.

FOR REFLECTION, DISCUSSION, AND ACTION

1. What verbal and visual cues do you use to determine if someone is listening to you? Which (if any) of these do you find challenging to maintain?

2. What do you know about the history of the writing center at your institution? Can you brainstorm a list of people within and outside of the writing center who might be good participants for an oral history project?

3. How would you respond as a researcher if your interview participant is saying something you disagree with or even find

offensive? In this situation, do you think the researcher's role would be to document, respond, or something else?

RECOMMENDED RESOURCES

Hesse-Biber, Sharlene Nagy, and Patricia Leavy. *The Practice of Qualitative Research.* 2nd ed. Thousand Oaks, CA: Sage, 2011. Print.

Mould, David. "Interviewing." *Catching Stories: A Practical Guide to Oral History.* Ed. Donna DeBlasio, Charles Ganzert, David Mould, Stephen Paschen, and Howard Sacks. Athens, OH: Ohio UP, 2009. Print. 82–103.

Rubin, Herbert, and Irene Rubin. *Qualitative Interviewing: The Art of Hearing Data.* 2nd ed. Thousand Oaks, CA: Sage, 2005. Print.

Smitherman, Carey. "Conducting an Oral History of Your Own Writing Center." *The Writing Lab Newsletter* 27.10 (2003): 1–4. PDF.

After the Study: *Emily Standridge*

Emily reflects on her doctoral research project that combined surveys, interviews, and observation that concluded in her dissertation "Characterizing Writing Tutorials."

For my dissertation project, I wanted to study the writing tutorial as an entity unto itself. There has been so much research into and theorizing about what happens around the tutorial but not enough work really focusing on what happens in the tutorial itself. I chose to do case studies, with the case being the individual tutorial, because there are so many contributing factors to each tutorial and the multiple data points that construct the case study allowed me to really dig into some of these various factors. I collected video recordings of the tutorials, written observations of the tutorials, surveys that assessed the level of engagement in the students and tutors during the tutorial (using flow theory), and interviews with student and tutor participants; then I used grounded theory to explore the characteristics common to tutorials and how those characteristics differed based on the level of engagement.

The interview data was a particularly great source of information on how both the student and the tutor experienced the tutorial. Interviews happened within one week of the tutorial for the students and within one month of the tutorial for the tutor (due to difficulties in tutors' availability to meet). Functionally, this meant that I interviewed student participants before the tutor participants, so with the tutors, I had more data available to direct their reflections on the experience of the tutorial. This data, in addition to the tutors' inherent increased interest in tutorials, resulted in much more reflection in their interviews.

While the tutors showed a lot more reflection on their sessions overall, one student's reflections during the interview stood out. This was a student who relied heavily on the writing center with almost weekly scheduled visits that often resulted in a follow-up appointment. Her repeat visits allowed her to think rather deeply about what made tutorials effective and engaging, something students who were first-time or infrequent users were not able to or had not done. There was some difficulty, though, in this student's ability to separate out one tutorial from another. Tutors had the same difficulty isolating individual meetings, especially when they had seen many students with the same assignment.

While both this student and all the tutors were able to recall the specifics of the tutorial being investigated given enough specific details from my observation notes, this difficulty in calling out individual tutorials was interesting in itself. It confirmed my belief that none of these tutorials was the model of engagement I had hoped to find, which did change the shape of the final dissertation. It also suggested that, while studying the tutorial as a case unto itself is a valuable enterprise, to get an optimum level of reflection on an individual tutorial, a more effective model would include observations of many meetings between the same student and tutor and interviews would happen after each tutorial as well as at the end of the data collection.

5 Studying Populations

I can't imagine a reader of this book who has not taken a survey before. In the United States, at least, we are bombarded with survey requests. We get them in emails, from campus offices, from employers, from political groups, on websites, on the phone, and we're even urged to take a survey on the bottom of many cash register receipts. Rarely a week goes by on the WCENTER or WPA-L listservs[11] without a plea from hopeful researchers asking readers to complete a survey. We likely have also encountered course evaluations, a type of survey, in our classes, and in many writing centers, tutors ask each client to complete a satisfaction survey at the end of a session.[12]

Surveying is a popular method for writing center researchers, in part, because it is cheap and quick. Surveys can be crafted online for free and sent by email to hundreds or thousands of people in minutes. Then, your data practically collects itself. For these reasons, it is very appealing to do a survey. Yet, as this chapter will discuss, a survey is not the answer to every research problem.

WHY SURVEY?

I've just suggested that surveying is quick, and perhaps by implication, easy. On the one hand, it's true. It's technically quick easy to create and distribute (especially online) surveys. Yet, on the other hand, this chapter will advise careful attention to planning, question-writing (also called instrument or questionnaire development), sampling, and recruitment so that your survey answers your research question and provides you with data that meets your needs.

A researcher generally uses a survey when he or she wants a big picture description of a population, particularly of the population's attitudes and beliefs as it is generally believed that this is what respondents can answer in a survey format. For example, if a researcher wants to know what first-year writers at a particular college think about the writing center, he or she might devise a survey to send to either the entire population (all of the first-year writers) or a sample (smaller subgroup) of the population. If researchers use random sampling, they may make generalizations about the population; that is, researchers could say something is very likely true for the entire population based on the survey of the sample. Surveys often also ask respondents for demographic characteristics in order for researchers to see the relationship or correlation between responses and characteristics. So, a study of student beliefs about the writing center might ask for, say, students to indicate their major to see if there is any significant relationship between major and response.

Though Peter Carino and Doug Enders suggest that writing center researchers prefer qualitative methods (83), surveying is a (mainly) quantitative method frequently used by writing center researchers. In fact, it was much easier when researching for this book to find published accounts of surveys than of other methods of writing center research. (Of course, this might have to do more with the difficulty of reducing qualitative data to article-sized pieces than surveying being the method of choice.) Still, the familiarity of surveying does mean that it is quite frequently used in studies as the only method of data gathering or as one method in a mixed-method study.

Surveys are limited to what respondents can and will respond to. A researcher can ask by survey how often a student used the writing center during his or her undergraduate years, but the student might not remember. A search of writing center records might be more accurate. Likewise, a researcher can ask a tutor by a survey how often she asked questions during her last session, but she likely did not keep track. Observation or recording a session will yield better results. Thus, consider carefully how well your respondents can provide you the answers you hope to find.

Surveys are helpful when personal accounts are available of a particular phenomenon, but the researcher wants to discover if the anecdotal account holds true for the larger population. For example, Karen Rowan used a nationwide survey (and follow up interviews) in her dissertation on graduate student writing center administrators because she wanted to know big picture if respondents would describe graduate student administrative positions as she had read and heard in anecdotal accounts. She writes:

> Although I, like many in the field, am drawn to narratives and value them as a way of making knowledge, I have nevertheless become frustrated with the anecdotal nature of many essays on graduate education and GSAs in particular. In too many cases, individual authors rely on anecdotal or narrative evidence drawn from only one context—that of the author's own program—to make broad claims about GSA positions or administrative professional development. (6)

Likewise, in their study on writing center student satisfaction, Carino and Enders use a specific term to describe the anecdotal accounts that Rowan is questioning—**lore**: "quantitative research does enable us to take more informed positions in our arguments, to add information to the intuitions, observations, hunches, suspicions, and guesses of daily experience that empower our lore" (101). Thus, they see surveys as one way to "test" assumptions on which we operate, to see if our own perspectives play out in the larger population.

Surveys do not have to be national or international in scope to be helpful. Wendy Bishop, for one, used a survey at her institution to question the appropriateness of required sessions. She finds from surveying students in twenty-two classes that required sessions do bring students to the center, and as a result, she decides to require a session for all first-year writers (39). In another survey study, Alicia Brazeau, a writing center tutor working in a writing fellows program, used a survey to gauge whether students preferred one-to-one or group feedback sessions. Her findings suggested that students found both approaches useful, a finding which will likewise inform future programmatic choices (49).

Ways to Survey

Should you determine that what you want to know is most appropriately ascertained by a survey, you'll have several other decisions to make simultaneously, each bearing influence on the other.

Scope: Local or Broader

Depending on what you hope to find out, you can decide if you want
to survey a local population or a broader population. If your question concerns just your own writing center, students or faculty at your
school, or anything community-specific, then you would survey locally. If your question concerns broader trends, then you can survey at the
city, state, regional, national, or international level. Irene Lurkis Clark,
in "Leading the Horse: The Writing Center and Required Visits," was
interested to know how required visits affected student perceptions
at her own center. Thus, she conducted a local study using a cluster
sample to select twenty-six of 155 sections of first-year writing (33).
She finds, similar to Bishop's survey mentioned above, that students
are more likely to attend the writing center if required to do so (34).

Since Rowan was less interested in what was happening specifically
at her center and more interested in what was happening around the
country, her survey was national in scope. But instead of sending her
survey to WCENTER or WPA-L, she carefully researched institutions
to target and mailed paper copies to particular schools. She describes
how she identified and recruited participants: "The study's population
included writing center directors and GSAs working in institutions
granting MA and/or PhD degrees in English studies (both with and
without rhetoric and composition graduate programs). I mailed survey
packets including one writing center director questionnaire and three
GSA questionnaires to 385 writing centers and received responses from
204 writing centers (52% response rate)" (2). For Rowan, her study
and recruitment strategies were appropriate for her research question.

Casting the largest possible net, Ellen Schendel crafted an international study to see how much time tutors spend on grammar in
sessions. She distributed the survey via listservs and had about 300
respondents. She finds that "just over half of the survey's respondents
(168 tutors) reported that they spend at least 26% of their tutoring
time working with writers on grammar and mechanics" (2). Thus, her
project was able to notice interesting trends globally. The scope of your
project should be determined by what you need to know. The temptation exists to turn every project into a national or international one, so
keep your intent in mind. If you want to use the results to influence
change in your own setting, then local numbers might be more per-
suasive than global ones.

Delivery Method: Online, By Mail, By
Phone, On Paper, Face-to-Face

The scope of your project will also influence how you will get your survey to possible respondents. If your project is local, it may be easiest to get paper copies to respondents (as Bishop does by having teachers distribute the surveys in class) or catch people for a face-to-face survey (such as students leaving the writing center or faculty in their offices). If your project is broader in scope, it is more practical to conduct your survey online, by mail, or by phone. All of these potential methods have benefits and drawbacks. For instance, mail can be expensive, but a survey by mail could stand out more than an email request. Face-to-face surveying is more time consuming, but you might get a higher completion rate than other types of self-administered surveys. In *Designing Surveys,* Ronald Czaja and Johnny Blair suggest you might expect a 45–75% completion rate for mailed survey, 60–90% for phone surveys, and 65–95% for face-to-face surveys (32). Further, they note that questions on face-to-face surveys can be more complex than other methods because the surveyor can clarify on the spot; however, respondents might be more willingly to respond to sensitive topics via mail (32).

Ad Hoc or Existing Survey

Most writing center researchers craft their own questionnaire, also known as a survey instrument, so I'll give you some advice in doing so, later in this chapter. However, that is not your only option with a survey project. You can use a survey instrument someone else crafted to see if you get similar results with a different population or at a different point in time. Czaja and Blair suggest that "[b]orrowing questions from other research studies is acceptable, even encouraged" (19). Likewise, there are many psychological survey instruments that are widely used to determine certain traits. For example, Beth Rapp Young and Barbara Fritzsche use Solomon and Rothblums's Procrastination Assessment Scale and Spielberger's State-Trait Anxiety Inventory in combination with their own survey in their study on procrastination (47–48). This allowed them to see correlations between students' likeliness to procrastinate and their likeliness to use the writing center. Similar options exist for other traits and tendencies though the instruments tend to be rather long. Especially if you are combining an existing instrument with your own, you will need very willing participants. Young and Fritzsche, who had participants complete three instruments in total, paid each participant ten dollars for their time (47).[13]

Generalizable or Not

Statistically speaking, there are surveys that you can generalize from and there are surveys that you cannot. If you need a survey about which you can say with some confidence that your findings are representative of the population studied, then you need to use a specific type of sampling called **random** or **probability sampling** and an adequate **response rate**. Let's look at an example: if you want to know if visitors to your center used feedback from their tutors in their revisions, you might want to send the questionnaire to all of your clients. But, let's say, you had 5,000 clients last year and that number is too large to work with in the timeframe you have for your project. So, instead, you decide to target a smaller subgroup of the population for the survey. For a sample to be random, each member of the population must have an equal chance of being selected to participate. If you select only the clients who came in November, only the clients whose last name begins with A, or only clients currently enrolled in a writing-intensive course, you have not given every member of the population an equal chance at being selected.

Most writing center survey projects do not use probability sampling and thus are not generalizable. Instead, writing center surveys often use **convenience sampling**—a sampling technique in which respondents self-select for participation. Take for example, Melissa Ianetta, Michael McCampley, and Catherine Quick's survey project reported in "Taking Stock: Surveying the Relationship of the Writing Center and TA Training." The authors designed their own questionnaire and distributed it via WCENTER and WPA-L. Though readership of these two mailing lists number in the thousands, they received just 28 usable responses (112). Their findings about teaching assistant training are interesting but clearly not generalizable both because of sampling technique and response rate. The authors instead use their findings to make suggestions for future research. Likewise, Kathleen Hunzer used a nonrandom sample in her study of perceptions of gender in the writing center. She sent the survey to seventy-four students and received thirty-nine responses to test her belief that students rated male tutors higher. Like Ianetta et al., Hunzer believes her study suggests an area where further research is necessary, even though she cannot generalize from her findings.

Single-Stage or Multi-Stage; Single Method or Mixed-Method

In crafting your survey project, you can also determine whether you will distribute a survey once or at several points to the same population or different populations. For example, in Julie Bauer Morrison and Jean-Paul Nadeau's survey project, they distribute three surveys to the same sample: one survey directly following a tutorial, one survey after the student received a grade on the project he/she took to the writing center, and one survey a full year later (28). This allows them to see that student satisfaction with the center was high directly following the session, lower after the grade was received, and then once again high a year later (31–32). Such findings would not be available to them if their survey was only administered once.

Researchers can also decide to mix a survey with other data points. Surveys used along with other data can provide baseline data for participants. Kelly Shea, in "Through the Eyes of the OWL: Assessing Faculty vs. Peer Tutoring in an Online Setting," uses a survey along with documents from OWL tutorials (digital comments on student texts) and conference summaries written by tutors (6). Since she was curious whether students would rate faculty and student tutors differently, she used a survey. But she was also curious if the tutorials were different enough (between faculty and student tutors) to warrant different student reactions, so the other data points helped fill in the picture in a way that just using survey data would not have.

PLANNING AND CONDUCTING

Populations and Sampling

The population is the entire group under study and the sample are the members of the larger group selected to participate in your study. The decision of what sample of the population to query with a survey depends on a number of factors. For example, if a population is known (or can be accurately found), such as the number of students currently enrolled in first-year writing at a college—then, based on the size of that population, it is possible to take a random sample (necessary if generalizing from the data is important). It is considered poor form to generalize—to suggest that the findings are typical of the whole population—if a researcher does not take a random sample. Say, for example, you just asked one first-year writing class that you were teaching if they knew about the writing center. Your findings could tell us what that one section knows, but you could not say that your class is representative.

To take a random sample, you would start by finding official counts of the population, if possible. Sometimes researchers, especially when they are researching a population to which they do not belong, do not have immediate access to the size of a population. However, there are not usually privacy issues related to knowing the size of a population, so you only need to track down the right person to ask for the data. (Like so many elements of research, this can take time and repeated efforts. Build this time into your timeline.) This list of all the members of a population (whether they are known to you by name, email, ID number, or random code) is your **survey frame**. With this frame, you can select a random sample.[14]

Often, populations ebb and flow within the timeframe of a study, so it is important to indicate the specific date and means by which the population was found in the report of the study. Additionally, in asking about population sizes, you might have to consider modifying your population. For instance, say you find a listserv boasts a population of 40,000 "members." However, suppose the administrator points out that 500 of those are duplicates (same person, different email addresses) and that 1,500 have permanent error return messages (meaning they never receive messages). The researcher might modify the definition of the population number from "members of the listserv" to "unique, active accounts," changing the population from N=40,000 to N=38,000.[15]

After quantifying the population, the next thing to do if seeking generalizable data is to find an optimal sample size within that population. This most easily done with a **sample size calculator**. These are found online (e.g., http://www.surveysystem.com/sscalc.htm) and will provide you the sample size appropriate for your study. For example, if I'm doing the study with the listserv population of 38,000 (N=38,000), I will need to select the **confidence level** and the **confi-**

dence interval that I feel is sufficient. The confidence interval is also known as the margin of error. Pollsters often disclose these numbers when discussing poll results; they'll report one candidate in the lead by a certain amount plus or minus three percent, say. The three percent is the confidence interval.

The confidence level says my findings for my sample are likely for the whole x percent of the time; a common confidence level for surveys is ninety-five percent. So, if I put into my sample size calculator that my population is 38,000 and I want a margin of error of 5 with a ninety-five percent confidence level, the calculator tells me I need a sample size of 380 participants. If, for the same population, I want a margin of error of two and ninety-nine percent confidence, I need a sample size of 3,750.[16]

Once you know your frame and the sample size, you can assign a number to each person in the frame and use a **random number generator** (e.g., www.random.org) to tell you which participants you should include in your sample. The random number generator will list random numbers—as many as you need—and you'll match the random list to the frame. So if you need 5 participants and the random numbers provided are 27, 6, 4, 33, and 8, you would look at the frame and see which names have those numbers. (This is essentially the same as pulling names out of a hat.) This type of random sampling is known as *straight random sampling* since every person in the population has an equal chance of being selected.[17]

There are often good reasons to use a different type of random sample—a *stratified random sample*—instead. In this approach, the frame is divided into groups according to some characteristic that you want to observe. Say, for instance, that you are doing a survey that involves writing center tutors at different types of schools and you want either to have equal numbers in your sample from different schools or you want your sample to be in proportion to the population. In this case, you could sort your population by tutors from four-year colleges, two-year colleges, and high schools. Since there are more writing center tutors at colleges and universities than high schools, you could decide to sample more from those groups than from the high school group.

Knowing the sample size and having a sample frame makes for the "cleanest" sort of random sample. However, in many cases, the population size under study isn't known to any degree of certainty or is so large that a frame is impossible to gather. In these situations, it may be possible to use *cluster sampling*. Cluster sampling works well for writing center studies where a set frame is often unavailable—there's no master list of all writing center directors, tutors, or clients around the world.[18] Should you want to survey tutors, you might begin by randomly selecting writing centers and then asking selected centers for a list of tutors. Likewise, if doing a classroom study, you can randomly select sections to participate in your study.[19]

In many fields, only surveys that utilize probability sampling will be considered valid; however, non-probability sampling (what I've called convenience sampling) is quite common in writing center studies and Rhetoric and Composition in general. This might be attributed to the fact that the populations under study in writing studies cannot be easily counted. For one, federal privacy laws prohibit teachers or administrators from distributing or posting student lists publicly. Likely, the use of nonprobability sampling might be attributed to the field's emphasis on qualitative research, a lack of knowledge about sampling techniques, or an ambivalence toward survey data and the associated positivism that turns attitudes and beliefs into numbers. For whatever reason, researchers currently can and do conduct and publish surveys that use nonprobability sampling. (I'm one of them, in fact.)

MacNealy distinguishes three types of non-probability sampling: convenience sampling, purposeful sampling, and snowball sampling (156). For convenience samples, the researcher sends a survey to an entire population and allows each member to decide whether or not to participate. In purposeful sampling, the researcher only recruits participants with a certain characteristic—say, for example, only those students who have visited the writing center more than once. Snowball sampling might start as purposeful sampling, when the researcher asks participants if they know another member of the population that has the same characteristic. Consider a situation where I want to send a survey to writing center directors who were in tenure-track positions and denied tenure. This is a pretty limited group, but sometimes people who have been through situations like this know others who have as well. In this case, I can accrue more participants as I go.

Recruitment

Whether you are randomly selecting or hand-picking people from your population to respond to your survey, you will have to put some effort into encouraging response. Some researchers plead, some describe the benefits to participants, and some offer prizes or money. Most IRBs will not approve a study where the prize or money is seen as coercive (and many researchers do not have the funds for a major prize anyway). Do be clear what your study is about and why you hope participants will take part. It also helps to try to reach participants three times and to provide a deadline for the closing of a survey. Keep in mind that if you are working with a random sample and the sample size calculator suggests, let's say 500 participants, you will likely need to ask 1,000 or even more members of a population to participate to reach the goal of a sample size of 500.

Question Writing

If you're like me, you have started taking many more surveys than you have finished. Personally, I might abandon surveys for any number of reasons, but top on my list for not finishing a survey is poorly written questions, followed closely by a survey that goes on and on (and on and on!). It would be rare for me to spend more than twenty minutes on a survey. I'm afraid this makes me a rather cranky survey-taker. However, from using surveys in my own research, I can see in the results that I'm not the only one. I've had respondents stop a survey halfway through and have had respondents write in for a survey answer, "I don't understand this question." As a survey writer, you want to try to avoid both of these situations as much as possible because it means missed opportunities to capture the data you want from (mostly) willing participants. Thus, there are three key questions to ask yourself when you craft survey questions: Is this question clear? Am I asking just one question at a time? And, can my respondents answer this question?

Surveys are typically provided to participants in absence of the researcher (an exception would be the less common phone or face-to-face survey). As such, the wording must make sense to respondents without any further explanation from you. Trouble can surface with acronyms, insider language, and words that have more than one meaning or connotation. Say for instance that you want to survey past clients at your school to see what changes they made to their writing projects after their writing center visit. You want to know if there were "local" or "global" changes, yet these terms might not be familiar to the students. Likewise, if you asked what they "revised" versus what they "edited" to get at global and local changes, they still might not be familiar with the distinctions that scholars in Rhetoric and Composition make between these terms. A better approach would be to ask what changes were made and provide choices or a blank for respondents to enter and then you can decide in your analysis which are global and which are local.

Sometimes surveys will ask questions that are difficult or impossible to answer. For instance, if you include two variables in one question, respondents might not know how to answer. Say you ask clients in a satisfaction survey this question: Were you greeted promptly when you entered the center and asked to make another appointment at the end of your session? If I'm a client and I was greeted promptly, but not asked to make another appointment, I don't know if I should answer yes or no. Further, as a researcher, if someone selects "no" you don't know if it was because of the former, the latter, or both.

Many times multiple choice questions do not give respondents the answer they need to answer. For instance in one of Julie Bauer Morrison and Jean-Paul Nadeau's survey questions in "How Was Your Session at the Writing Center," they ask:

When did you go? Check any that apply.

A. The day the paper was due,

B. The day before,

C. The weekend before,

D. The week before. (40)

If a respondent went two weeks before, what does she select? Or, if the student goes on Friday before the paper is due, is that answer C or is it D? An easy solution to this sort of problem is to provide an option for "other" to questions where your might not be able to anticipate all of the possible answers.

Some survey questions also ask questions that a respondent may be in no position to know (e.g., How did your writing center begin?) or may ask for respondents to try to rely on long forgotten memories (e.g., In your first week of tutoring, did you work with any clients on comma use?). Some surveys will also ask respondents to estimate noncount items into quantitative terms. For example in Morrison and Nadeau's survey, they ask "What percentage of the advice you were offered did you use when revising your paper? 0% 10% 20% 30% 40% 50% 60% 70% 80% 90% 100%" (40). Unless the student is looking at a list of all of the advice offered, this will be quite difficult to do. Needless to say, your questions need to be answerable.

Types of Questions

One decision you'll need to make is whether you will have closed, open-ended, or both types of questions, and this decision should be based on what kind of data you want and what you want to do with the data. With closed questions, you provide the respondent the options to select. For example, the questionnaire in Wendy Bishop's article "Bringing Writers to the Center," has this closed question:

Approximately how many times have you been to the writing center this semester?

A. Never

B. 1–3 times

C. 3–6 times

D. More than 6 times. (42)

This type of question will give you consistent data from respondents that you can count. Online survey programs will, in fact, provide frequencies and percentages for this type of data automatically.

Open-ended questions allow for respondents to provide their own responses. Bishop's questionnaire also has open-ended questions like this one: "From your experience, what is the best, most supportive, and least threatening method for the Writing Center and writing teachers to use to get students to the Writing Center?" (42). Open-ended questions let respondents use their own words and might provide answers that you did not or could not anticipate. For example, one of Bishop's respondents wrote "give them bad grades" to this question, which, I'm guessing, is not something that Bishop would have provided as a multiple choice response (43).

Some surveys, including Bishop's, have hybrid questions that are both closed and open-ended. One of hers is:

Would you recommend the center to other campus writers?

A. Yes

B. No

Explain. (42)

Obviously, a question like this will provide numerical data and descriptive data.

How Long?

Many writing center survey projects use primarily closed questions in combination with a few open-ended questions, often at the end (for example, see Bishop; Morrison and Nadeau; Ianetta, McCamley, and Quick; Brazeau). The percentage of closed to open-ended seems about 75 to 90 percent closed to 25 to 10 percent open-ended. These projects have from about ten to thirty questions overall. I suggest this to note a trend, not to provide a formula for survey design. Your own projects will vary based on your research question. Yet, when I coach students in their research projects, I suggest trying to keep to under twenty survey questions. Invested respondents will complete a survey with more than twenty questions, but it's a rare study in which all of your respondents are very invested in your project.

Sometimes researchers include items that unnecessarily make the survey longer. Depending on the purpose of the study, it may be necessary to ask demographic information—sex, age, race, home language—but there are times when this information is really not needed because it won't be used in the analysis. Since many surveys begin asking this information, sometimes researchers tend to include these just as a default. Ask yourself if this is really necessary. Additionally, using a hybrid open/closed-ended question where a respondent is asked "why?" after every response also increases the length of the survey. Or, in other cases, researchers get excited about administrating the survey and decide to throw in off-topic questions to seize the moment (i.e., While I have you here, can you also tell me about x, y, and z?). In my experience as a researcher, when the survey is too long, respondents begin to skip questions, or, perhaps, and this is more difficult to know, stop reading questions and just click through to get to the end.

How do you know if your survey is too long? Ask several people to test your survey. Some survey programs, like Survey Monkey, will tell you how long a respondent took to complete the survey. I don't think you can expect strangers or near strangers to give you more than twenty to thirty minutes of their time. Moreover, I've had the most success with surveys where I can assure respondents it will only take ten to fifteen minutes to complete.

Another consideration to make is the order of questions. Group questions by topics. Consider even using subheadings to indicate topics to readers. The order of topics isn't terribly important in all surveys, but MacNealey suggests that respondents will more likely tolerate and answer sensitive questions if they come later in the survey (153). Leading a survey with a question like "How often do you question your ability to tutor?" could put your respondents in a defensive stance or could lead respondents to drop the survey before beginning.

LIMITATIONS AND ETHICAL CONSIDERATIONS

Surveys are wonderful at pointing to trends in population, yet they are limited by participation and concerns of validity. Further, surveys in writing studies are often followed-up with interviews to get more human touch, more in-depth answers.

Of the strategies explored in this book, surveys, you might imagine, are less likely to be unethical because survey respondents' identities are often anonymous to even the researcher. However, survey researchers still need to be concerned with fairness in response and representation. For one, researchers can allow, when appropriate, for the option of "other" with space for an open-ended response rather than forcing respondents to select one of the researcher's choices.[20] Additionally, sometimes survey respondents will disclose something that makes them identifiable even when we've carefully crafted our questions and protocol to prevent identification. In these cases, you may strip identifying information out of responses.

Reporting ethically is likewise important. First, be sure not to generalize from your findings if you have not used a random sample. Second, be fair about what you do with the numbers. At my institution, faculty were recently surveyed about morale and employee satisfaction. Morale was low because salaries were documented as the lowest in the region. The president, in addressing the faculty about this issue, told us that if we took out nontenure track faculty and counted the efforts to raise salary (that were proposed but not yet reality) we would be within ten percent of the second lowest school. This sort of number wizardry—cutting out parts from the data that are unsavory—did not raise faculty morale. In reporting your research, you might be tempted to cut out a part of your findings that get in the way of the point you'd like to make. Resist this urge. Finally, as a reader, I like to see the exact wording of questions and answer options when a researcher is discussing a survey. Consider including full questions within the text or the full instrument at the end of the study in an appendix.

SUMMARY OF KEY POINTS: SURVEYING

- Surveys can reveal trends in populations, which are not obvious on the individual level.
- Survey researchers must decide whether or not generalizable data is important to know whether or not to take a random sample.
- Crafting surveys carefully can make the difference in the number of completed surveys and the success of the study.

FOR DISCUSSION, REFLECTION, AND ACTION

1. What is the worst survey you have started or completed? What made it so terrible?

2. What kinds of questions make you uneasy in surveys? What is your response (e.g., not answer, quit the survey, lie, or skip the question)?

3. What's one thing you would love to know from all users of your writing center? How about from all tutors? All faculty?

RECOMMENDED RESOURCES

Czaja, Ronald and Johnny Blair. *Designing Surveys.* 2nd Ed. Thousand Oaks, CA: Sage, 2004. Print.
MacNealey, Mary Sue. *Strategies for Empirical Research in Writing.* Boston, MA: Longman, 1998.

After the Study: *Karen Rowan*

Karen writes about what she learned during her dissertation project that resulted in two articles: "Beyond the Anecdotal: Questioning Assumptions about Graduate Student Administrators" and "All the Best Intentions: Graduate Student Administrative Professional Development in Practice."

I've learned through experience that survey research is trickier than it lets on. Surveys are so common that it's easy to be lulled into thinking that doing survey research is straightforward. Just come up with the questions, send it out, et voilà: research! Granted, sometimes surveys can be straightforward. More often, what's easy is designing a bad survey that frustrates participants and disappoints the researcher. I've learned this through experience, too.

When it came time to design my dissertation research, I heeded the lessons of my first run-in with surveys and spent time learning more about how to design them. I wrote about some of this in the articles based on my dissertation, and I think what I learned helped my project.

What's not so obvious from my articles is how I handled and analyzed my survey data and how unprepared I felt for those tasks. When I proposed my dissertation, I planned to use Excel for analysis: I knew SPSS was the better option, but I couldn't afford $1,500+ for software that I'd probably only use once. I also proposed to analyze correlations between different variables. What I didn't write was, "I have little idea what that means and even less of an idea of how I'll do it." Though I'd done months of preparation, immersing myself in the literature on research methods and on mentorship and graduate student administrators, I nevertheless found myself starting before I felt entirely ready and hoping to figure it out as I went along.

Fortunately, by the time I was collecting data, I was working at a nonprofit that had a copy of SPSS software that I could use, and, even better, some of my colleagues were doctoral students in education who understood statistics. Working with SPSS fundamentally changed the course of my research. The process of entering data from paper surveys, though tedious, gave me ample time to think about the responses and develop questions for the analysis phase. In effect, I started figuring out what kinds of "correlations" I wanted to know more about. When the time came, I had some questions worked out and was able to consult with a colleague to figure out what kinds of analyses to run in SPSS and what the results meant. That process resulted in the analyses that became the central focus of the "All the Best Intentions" article— and would not have been possible had I stuck to my original plan.

Nearly ten years later, I find myself in a similar place: I'm now working on assessment research for my university's directed self-placement program, work that has me designing surveys, using SPSS, and trying to understand statistics again. I continue to work at improving the design of my surveys, to set goals without knowing how I'm going to accomplish them, and to seek out colleagues with expertise that I lack. What's changed, perhaps, is that I'm more comfortable now with the idea that I'll always be learning as I go, diving in before I feel ready, and learning with and from others along the way.

6 Studying Sites and Tools

Contemporary post-process composition theory is marked by attention to both contexts (historical and material) and locations. Scholars in Rhetoric and Composition, more or less, agree that writing cannot be understood or taught acontextually. Writing does not sprout deep inside a writer's heart or mind without any influence from the world, nor does a reader come to a text without influence from the texts she has read before, history, genre, medium, material conditions, or physical location. When we read and when we write, we participate in a complex human activity that is interconnected to other human activities; thus, even when done alone, reading and writing are social acts. Since we understand writing or communication as influenced by and representations of cultures to which we might belong, many contemporary composition researchers set out not to study individual writers, but the contexts in which the writers operate.

The key method for studying writers in context is **fieldwork** (also called **participant observation** or simply **observation**). Fieldwork is time spent in the participants' own contexts (also know as being "in the field"), taking notes, paying attention, and, in some cases, interacting or participating in ongoing activities. This chapter explores how to do fieldwork as it is a method used as an essential data point in ethnography and autoethnography and is also used in many case studies and usability studies. Each of these types of studies and how they use fieldwork will be discussed in this chapter.

WHY DO FIELDWORK?

If we want to learn about an activity that is place-based, it makes sense to go to the place where the activity happens. Thus, if our activity is writing center work, we may go to writing centers. Of course, much writing center work happens in other sites too, including but not limited to virtual spaces. Many readers of this book may already spend many hours a week in a writing center or other spaces where writing center work happens, but entering a space to do fieldwork is different; it changes our relationship to the space, people, and activities. In doing fieldwork, we pay attention to how people interact, and, in ethnographic studies, we take notice of how cultures cohere. We can learn about rituals, rules, typical behaviors, materials, and language use from spending extended periods of time in the space (Chiseri-Strater and Sunstein 94). Fieldwork is the primary method for naturalistic research, which is research that comes closest to studying "natural" behaviors of participants. Fieldwork is primarily watching and taking notes on participants engaged in their everyday experiences; it may also include recording, participating, activity logging, and spontaneous interviewing (or just engaging in conversations and asking questions).

TYPES OF STUDIES THAT USE FIELDWORK

Ethnography

Ethnography is the study of a culture, an approach with roots in anthropology but now widely adapted to other fields. Fieldwork is the primary method of ethnography. Ethnographers spend hours, days, weeks, months, and sometimes even years observing and taking notes in the field. Additionally, ethnographers interact and even participate in the activities at their sites to better understand the **emic perspective** of the culture at hand and to become familiar and accepted by insiders at the site. Emic perspective is the insider perspective, in contrast with an **etic perspective,** which is a universal or outsider perspective. From combining their observations and notes, with interviews, artifact or discourse analysis, and historical research, ethnographers aim to make visible the "seemingly invisible networks" affecting participants (Sheridan 73).

To tease out the difference in the types of studies that use fieldwork, let's imagine we have an aerial view of a site we want to study, and we have spotlights we can use to illuminate as needed. If we were conducting an ethnography, we would have the entire site lit. For in ethnography, every person, artifact, document, conversation, tool, and action within the site is potentially meaningful to understand and may help render a representation of the site or the culture under study. Thus, the challenge of ethnography is probably immediately apparent—the ethnographer tries to see everything—and, this is the hard part—stay aware of everything even as activities become normalized. Yet, the all-encompassing gaze is also the benefit of ethnography. Nothing is off-limits or dismissed from the start as unimportant. Or, as Kathy Charmaz asks herself, "What should an ethnographer study in the field?" and responds, "Whatever is happening there" (21).

Several writing center scholars have noted how ethnography is an excellent strategy for studying writing center work. For one, Tom Hemmeter and Carolyn Mee think ethnography (or an ethnographic perspective) can help remind us that "tutorials do not occur on a Platonic cloud" (4). They write, "The writing center involves not just a simple, one-on-one, private conversation. In fact, the typical writing center conference is a complex, multi-directional, dynamic conversation" (4). Thus, if we analyze the talk of writing center conferencing without considering the many influences on that talk, we might reach naive understandings. Further, Janice Neulieb and Maurice Scharton like that ethnography acknowledges the personhood and the subjectivities of the researcher. They think other research methods make claims to objectivity that they can't keep (56). Ethnography for writing center research, instead, is more credible if only when ethnographers use "meticulous and comprehensive record keeping" (57).

Since ethnography often implies long-term time commitments and complete cultural immersion, there are few published accounts of writing center research that calls itself ethnography proper. However, many writing center studies use ethnographic perspectives and/or tools even if they are not "true" ethnographies. As David Sheridan observes, J. Green and David Bloome demarcate the difference between doing ethnography versus *adopting an ethnographic perspective* (studying particular aspects of a culture instead of all aspects), and *using ethnographic tools* (doing some fieldwork combined with interviews or activity logs) (80). For example, Terese Thonus in "Triangulation in the Writing Center" calls her approach "a qualitative, ethnographic methodology combining participant observation with informant interviews" (62). And, Tom Reigstad labels his dissertation project and the subsequent publication from that study in which he observed forty writing conferences "ethnographic."

Neal Lerner also conducted an ethnographic dissertation. As he describes in "Insider as Outsider: Participant Observation as Writing Center Research," using a center for his research where he worked made things complicated. His working role shifted from near peer (he was a senior tutor) to "observer and evaluator" (53). Subsequently, participants were slow to fulfill promises. Still, with interviews, observation, and his own research memos, he was able to see his center in different (if not "new") ways and he recommends ethnography and ethnographic projects for other writing center researchers.

Autoethnography

Autoethnography is a type of ethnography (also sometimes called critical or new ethnography) in which the researcher plays a central role as both investigator and subject of the research. Instead of trying, as in traditional ethnography, to see and report the happenings of a culture as an outsider, an autoethnographer operates from a consciously subjective perspective. The autoethnographer does not try to tell the story of another's culture, but rather believes he or she can only tell her story within a culture. In this way, the autoethnographer resists, to some degree, making representations of others.

If we zoom out to our imaginary aerial view again, in the case of autoethnography, a spotlight would follow the researcher around the research site. The autoethnographer is the subject of a study to the degree that his or her feelings and thoughts can be recorded as data. As Suresh Canagarajah notes, "The researcher/subject roles are fused" (114). Autoethnography is one of the newer research strategies for Rhetoric and Composition; as such, the dimensions and norms of autoethnography have yet to solidify. Canagarajah describes three types ranging from a more traditional ethnographic approach where the researcher also writes about him or herself in the study to an approach which seems nearly indistinguishable from a personal essay (117).

Meesh McCarthy and Erin O'Brien use autoethnography to explore their roles as writing center tutors in their article "Check One: Tutor Hat, Teacher Hat, Facilitator Hat, Some/All/None of the Above." They find the strategy provides flexibility in the complex story they have to tell. They write, "This is not a narrative which provides an all-encompassing and exhaustive ethnography or autobiography of the writing center tutor. It is a disjointed invitation for readers to wear their multiple hats while reading this text" (29). Similarly, Lauren Schiely uses autoethnography to understand stories told about writing center work in her project, "Sharing Our Stories: Using Narrative Inquiry to Examine Our Writing Centers." In both cases, the authors make compelling cases for how autoethnography can expand our received understandings about writing center work and relationships.

Case Study

Case study researchers select particular participants as "cases," people or perhaps groups or classes, to profile in depth within the population or setting. Whereas an ethnographer watches an entire scene, case study researchers focus their gaze on just their cases. So, in the imaginary aerial view, there would be perhaps four to eight spotlights focused on the cases selected by the participant; the light might follow the cases outside of the setting as well. (However, case studies do not always include fieldwork in the setting; as mentioned earlier, case studies typically combine multiple methods that often but not always include fieldwork.) Like ethnography, case studies collect several points of data; most often data includes interviews, artifact or discourse analysis, and fieldwork or surveying. You might hear a case study described as "ethnographic" when it includes fieldwork so that the researcher can contextualize the findings of the case in the larger setting.

Case studies are a very popular form of writing center research. Like autoethnography, there is a vein of case study research that is closer to essay or practitioner inquiry than to research as defined here. In this type of "case study" the author tells the story of one or more cases (experiences) as an after the fact reflection (e.g., see Joyce Kinkead and Jeanette Harris's collection *Writing Centers in Context: Twelve Case Studies*.) For the most part, however, case studies in writing center studies include planned, systematic collection of data. The most famous case in writing center studies, perhaps, is Fannie in Anne Dipardo's " 'Whispers of Coming and Going': Lessons from Fannie." Dipardo writes about Fannie after a semester-long study of a tutoring program. She decides to focus on Fannie and Fannie's tutor's work together, because she writes, "it is neither unusual or typical, but because it seems so richly revealing of the larger themes I noted again and again during my months of data collection—as unresolved tensions tugged continually at a fabric of institutional good intentions, and as tutors and students struggled, with ostensible good will and inexorable frustration, to make vital connection" (126). Dipardo's telling of the relationship between Fannie and her tutor shows just how compelling research involving sustained fieldwork can be.

A more recent case study project is Stephen Corbett's "Using Case Study Multi- Methods to Investigate Close(r) Collaboration: Course-Based Tutoring and the Directive/Nondirective Instructional Continuum." In this project, Corbett uses

> a combination of rhetorical and discourse analyses and ethnographic and case study multi-methods to investigate both the scenes of teaching and learning—planning between tutors and graduate teaching assistants (TAs) and participant interactions in the classroom and during one-to-one tutoring sessions—as well as the points of view and interpretations from all the participating actors in these scenes: two TAs, two peer tutors, twenty students, and one researcher. (57)

Through observation, recordings, surveys, artifact analysis, and interviews, Corbett juxtaposes tutors doing class-based tutoring and in-center tutoring, which provides an excellent model for other researchers wanting to know how to balance multiple data points.

Usability Testing

A type of case study that can use fieldwork is usability testing. **Usability testing** is typically the study of how users use a tool, often a technology. Usability testing is sometimes conducted as an experiment in a usability lab, but in writing studies, and in particular in writing center studies, usability testing is often more qualitative and naturalistic. The idea is to observe how users use a particular tool (or website or even document) to understand how it could be improved upon. Usability testing is used extensively in technical writing and Web design. Sometimes users are asked by researchers to complete particular tasks using the site, tool, or document; other times users are simply observed using the site, tool, or document in their daily work or play. Fieldwork in these studies is typically strictly observational, not participatory.[21] In our imaginary aerial view, like case study in general, particular people (or "users") would be lit only when they are engaging with the tool, site, or document in question.

Usability testing with fieldwork is an aspect of several writing center studies. For example, Amber Buck's article, "The Invisible Interface: MS Word in the Writing Center," is a case study with a usability aspect to it because she studied how writing center tutors work with students on desktops and laptops (instead of paper copies). What becomes apparent in her observations is that Microsoft Word becomes a third voice in the sessions that students found difficult to ignore—drawing student attention to "errors" with squiggly lines. Buck uses observation along with video and screen capture in her study. Similarly, Tammy Conard-Salvo and John M. Spartz use fieldwork in their usability study published in "Listening to Revise: What a Study about Text-to-Speech Software Taught Us about Students' Expectations for Technology Use in the Writing Center" to pay attention to how tutors and students make use of a technology called Kurzweil 3000. Since writing center work involves many sites, tools, and documents, there are many possible avenues to explore with usability studies.

Planning and Conducting

Selecting a Site

The primary challenge when planning fieldwork for ethnography or autoethnography is site selection. Though there is a tendency to want to study sites we are familiar with or that are in close proximity to us, those sites, in ways, can be more difficult to study. Ethnography and autoethnography require us to pay attention to the ordinary, unremarkable, routine aspects of a site, activity, or culture. If we have a familiarity with a site, activity, or culture, these ordinary aspects become invisible to us. We simply stop seeing them—the same way our eyes see our nose on our face but our brain filters out that stimulus. So, if we select a site that is familiar to us or a culture to which we belong (or even sites or cultures that are similar to ones we are familiar with) we have to **denaturalize** the activities in our minds to pay attention and make good observations. Denaturalizing is seeing ordinary things anew, paying close attention to the everyday, expected, and naturalized assumptions we have about how people operate in their worlds.

Permissions

Though you are welcome to observe and even record "public" sites and events, most writing center studies will not happen in public locations. (Some schools and campuses, in fact, will prohibit recording anywhere without permission.) Regardless, it is always best research practice to be upfront and get permission for your observation plans. If you are doing fieldwork in a writing center, you will need the permission of the director. (Likewise, at any other site, you will need the permission of the person in charge.) You will not need permission (consent forms) from every single person who enters the site, but if the person becomes prominent in your observations, do talk to him or her about your study. In a classroom study, however, you will want consent from all students. Those who do not give you consent should not be showcased in your reporting. Regardless of your site, it is very important that you be upfront about your role; covert observations are inappropriate and unfair.

Time in the Field

The time spent devoted to fieldwork depends on the type and the scope of your project. If you are doing fieldwork as part of an ethnography or autoethnography, you will spend extended periods of time doing fieldwork. For a small-scale project, sometimes called a mini- or micro-ethnography, you might spend just a few hours a day for a few weeks in the field—maybe twenty to forty hours in the field. It takes some time to discern what is ordinary for a particular space or culture and what is not. Larger projects require more observations. One particularly notable ethnography is *Ways with Words: Language, Life and Work in Communities and Classrooms* by Shirley Brice Heath. Heath spent over a decade conducting fieldwork (and then three decades doing a generational, follow-up study!). Many ethnographies in Rhetoric and Composition are classroom-based and thus span only one semester. If you are doing fieldwork for a case study or usability test, you'll likely observe for more limited time periods with a more focused gaze. As noted above, you'll be more interested in how your cases function or how a particular tool is used rather than trying to get a sense of the whole context in which the participants operate.

Taking Fieldnotes

The notes you take while observing (or soon after observing if the site/
conditions do not allow for note taking) are a key data point. If you
take lousy notes, you'll have lousy data to use for your study even if you
spent hours and hours in the field doing observations. Fieldnotes take
practice. It isn't easy to decide where to focus your gaze, what to record, and to continue to pay attention as the days and weeks progress.

Several scholars give recommendations on what to record and how
to record fieldnotes. Here are a few suggestions:

Kathy Charmaz:

- Record individual and collective actions
- Emphasize significant processes happening
- Take note of what participants define as interesting or
  problematic
- Note language use
- Place actors/actions in context (22)

Elizabeth Chiseri-Strater and Bonnie Sunstein:

- Number and date each page of notes; include time and place
  of observation
- Record sensory details
- Use description, not value judgments
- Note follow up questions (120)

Blakeslee and Fleischer:

- Pay attention to how people interact
- Record what people do in the setting
- Record how they respond or react to experiences
- Note what happens regularly and sporadically
- See how the setting is organized and structured
- Pay particular attention to what changes (110)

There are not right and wrong ways to take fieldnotes. In many
settings, you may be able to use a laptop, tablet, or other device for
taking notes; however, in some settings—especially where you are expected to participate—that would be untenable. Still, you may be able

to have a notebook or even a small piece of paper in your pocket for occasional scribbles if other devices won't work. In certain settings, it will make your participants uncomfortable for you to take any notes. In these cases, you will have to write from memory when you return from the field.

Many who take fieldnotes in field use a double entry system. On the left side they will record what is happening (all of the things suggested by the scholars above). On the right side, they will note their impressions and feelings and questions about what is going on. Using this sort of system encourages reflection and interpretation and helps you know later what actually happened and what you thought about it. On a similar note, many devise shorthand for common words or people in the field.

Additional Fieldwork Data

In addition to observing and taking notes, fieldwork can also involve sketching, activity logging, recording, document analysis, and active participation. Researchers will often do sketching in the field. I typically draw a crude floor plan when I first enter the field. In classroom observations, I will sometimes draw squares for each student desk or seat in relation to where the teacher sits. I sometimes code the seats (S1 for Student 1, S2 for Student 2 and so on) so I can connect the students in my notes with where they sat during my observations even before I know their names. I sometimes also track the movements of people using the map I craft at the beginning.

Some fieldwork researchers also keep an activity log.[22] Activity logs are preprinted documents with a list of behaviors down one side that you want to keep track of. Across the top are time ranges or individuals within the field. A simple example might be that I want to pay attention to how many tutoring sessions are happening at six times throughout the day. So the behavior is "tutoring" and I list my six times across the top. I visit during those times and count the number of sessions I see.

Field researchers will also use recordings. Shirley Brice Heath made hours and hours of recordings during her decade-long ethnography. The recordings are most useful when they are just a conversation or interview of two or maybe three individuals (for audio) or a small group for video. Any more than that and it is difficult to transcribe and thus make much use of the recordings. (See Chapter 4 for more on recording.)

Most field researchers will also collect artifacts or documents that help them to understand the site. Classroom ethnographers, for example, almost always collect course materials and ask for access to digital course sites. For writing center field research when the site is a writing center, you might want to see if the writing center has current or older documents related to your study. Many writing centers have informal archives in the form of old filing cabinets or a central computer with all pertinent files. Many field researchers take photographs as well to help them remember the site after they leave the field, and, with permissions, to use in the research report. For Sarah Pink, photographs are key to what she calls visual ethnography, a type of fieldwork not yet popular in writing center studies.

Finally, many field researchers participate within the scene. Wendy Bishop recommends writing studies researchers take on the role of active observer. They should, she writes, try "moving into the scene where it seems natural and polite, and moving back to observe more carefully when that also seems functional" (Bishop 75). However, Chiseri-Strater and Sunstein stress that there's a limit to how much you can participate and still do your research. They say you cannot "do ethnography" while teaching your own classes and I agree (Chiseri-Strater and Sunstein 95). When you are orchestrating an activity it is impossible to be a sponge on the side soaking up the scene.

LIMITATIONS AND ETHICAL CONSIDERATIONS

The greatest limitation of fieldwork is what Emerson, Fretz, and Shaw call the researcher's "consequential presence" (3). That is the impact of the researcher on the field. Will they act "normal" with you observing? However, Emerson, Fretz, and Shaw argue their presence is not a contamination of the site (3). The researcher makes an impact on the site, yes, but it can be useful to see how you are treated as a researcher and thus learn how outsiders or newcomers are initiated into the site.

Mary Sue MacNealey also notes that field research can have the potential for sampling error. This would be a problem of making interpretations on too narrow a set of observations—from only observing on Tuesdays, say, or just mornings or only using talkative people for informants (224–25). Field researchers should try to offset the potential for this error by spending a lot of time in the field and varying observations times and days. Further, MacNealey warns against researcher bias (225). Humans tend to make quick judgments and maintain them, sometimes leading to mistaken observations.[23]

Finally, field research like any other research that uses human participants, is a tricky art. You may observe situations that you'd rather not observe because of how it might throw off what you assumed about a site or because of your affinity for the people in the site. You might feel your representation of the participants in your write up is fair, but they might disagree or even be hurt. (There is some advice about including participants in your analysis and interpretation stage in Chapter 7, which can help with this.) Though you would never create an impression that was not in your data to make participants happy or keep the peace, you can always decide not to use data from a participant in your reporting if the situation seems too sticky.

Summary of Key Points: Fieldwork

- Fieldwork is time spent watching participants in their natural settings.
- Fieldwork requires a researcher to denaturalize a scene: to look at it as if he or she had never seen something like it before.
- Projects using fieldwork (ethnography, autoethnography, case studies, and usability studies) can last years, but can be briefer.
- When a researcher is "in the field" for an extended period and the notes, sketches, interviews, and logs are comprehensive, the research report will have more credibility.

For Discussion, Reflection, and Action

1. Think of your wider network: where might you be able to do fieldwork that helps answer your research question?

2. What tools are used by tutors at your writing center for tutoring or other writing center work? Do any of these tools cause problems for tutors or clients? How might you investigate writing center tool use with a usability study?

3. In your next class or meeting, try taking fieldnotes as if you
    were an outsider to the group. Pay attention to the advice given
    by scholars in this chapter on what to record. What do you
    notice from this experience? How did it change your normal
    experience in that class or group?

Recommended Resources

Bishop, Wendy. *Ethnographic Writing Research: Writing it Down, Writ-
    ing it Up, and Reading It.* Portsmouth, NH: Boynton/Cook, 1999.
    Print.
Chiseri-Strater, Elizabeth, and Bonnie Sunstein. *What Works? A Prac-
    tical Guide for Teacher Research.* Portsmouth, NH: Heinemann,
    2006. Print.
Emerson, Robert, Rachel Fretz, and Linda Shaw. *Writing Ethnographic
    Fieldnotes.* Chicago, IL: U of Chicago P, 1995. Print.

After the Study: *Amber M. Buck*

Amber reflects on her research project completed originally for her master's thesis, which she then published as "The Invisible Interface: MS Word in the Writing Center" in the journal Computers and Composition.

One of the biggest challenges about researching writing technologies is how they change so quickly. Looking back at my *Computers and Composition* article and the larger thesis project it came from, I'm most struck by my emphasis on the desktop computer session, which feels rather quaint now. The challenge with research about technology is the ability to use one's findings to move beyond the specifics of that particular tool to draw larger conclusions about the nature of writing, teaching, and technology as a whole. I hope this research still resonates and that the conclusions I drew can be applied to other writing technologies. While tutoring sessions may include more laptops and tablets along with keyboards, mice, and yes, pencils and paper, it is even more important to pay attention to the materiality of the tutoring session and to consider how best to use those specific tools to assist the writer.

Microsoft Word has gone through several versions since I conducted this research, but its ubiquity has kept it as one of the most prominent tools used for writing. There are others, though, that provide writing tutors with different software options and more specialized tools to help writers: Scrivener, DevonThink, Evernote, and many more offer new opportunities to organize ideas and manage the writing process in ways that Microsoft Word cannot. The possibilities expand even further if we consider tools to help writers organize research: Digital writing researchers have discussed the importance of other writing tools beyond word processing for writing and research (Hensley Owens and Van Ittersum, 2013; Van Ittersum, 2009). Attention to other tools and their possibilities for writing tutoring is important now as well. End-Note, Zotero and others provide tutors with opportunities to assist writers with research writing in new ways also. Digital writing scholars have also created software tools themselves, most notably Eli Review (created by Grabill, Hart-Davidson, McLeod) and The Writing Studio (by Palmquist).

If I conducted a similar research project again, I would take a wider view of writing technologies within the tutoring session, to ensure the study's greater relevance beyond the specific technologies I examined. An aspect of this study that I believe still has relevance, though, are the multiple modes through which I conducted my analysis: talk, text, and interactions with the technology itself. To examine the influence of technologies within teaching and writing, using multiple methods and gathering data through multiple means provides the researcher with a more detailed picture of a particular technology. This approach is one I continue to use in my research of other writing technologies within writers' literacy practices.

7 Studying Possibilities: Action Research

In action research, truth is in the process of inquiry itself. Was it reflexive and dialectical? Was it ethical, democratic, and collaborative? Did participants learn new research skills, attain greater self-understanding, or achieve greater self-determination? Did it solve significant practice problems or did it contribute to our knowledge about what will not solve these problems? Were problems solved in a manner that enhanced the overall learning capacity of the individuals or system? These are the types of questions that guide action research. They are unlike those that guide most research.

—Linda Dickens and Karen Watkins

The beauty of qualitative research is how it can provide a richly detailed understanding of a research setting, subject, or phenomenon. It answers the ever-fascinating question: *what is happening here?* In reporting on research (which will be discussed in Part III), researchers can responsibly make suggestions for change or improvements, but that is where most research stops. For example, if I find in studying first-year writing center directors that new writing center directors spend inordinate amounts of time with record-keeping and internal reporting, I can make suggestions for the individuals in my study to discuss the problem with their mentors and superiors, and I can suggest that writing center scholars and professionals think about how we fetishize number-crunching. However, I cannot actually make changes for the first-year directors because I cannot responsibly generalize from my qualitative data from a few cases to say something is nationally a serious issue, and, importantly, I am not a part of their immediate campus contexts where I could enact changes. That we have methods to systematically describe a research setting, subject, or phenomenon is helpful, but sometimes description does not feel adequate when we are confronted with serious issues.

Action research is an approach to qualitative research that begins with the intention to identify and confront problems through enacting change in the researcher's own community. In this way, action research is an appealing type of qualitative research because it does not conclude with mere suggestions but rather puts solutions to self-identified problems into motion. In many ways, I'd argue, action research is an orientation to research that makes it closely aligned with often expressed values of writing center practice. For one, action research is often seen as a path to conjoin theory and practice, prioritizing neither. Likewise, writing centers are often seen as sites where theories about writing and teaching writing are put into practice and refined. Moreover, action research and writing center work both tout reflexivity as a core practice and each insist upon the importance of being grounded in the local setting. Even so, writing center researchers have published very few accounts of action research.[27]

Nonetheless, many who work in writing centers already engage in some of the behaviors associated with action research. For instance, a writing center tutor who notices several students struggling with the writing assignments from a particular class might start mentally cataloging these students. She might ask other tutors if they have seen the same issue. She might ask questions of the struggling students that she reports back to the whole staff at a staff meeting or she might make a note in her end of the session documentation for her director about what she's noticed. Together, the staff might think of a way to address the problem and they might report back on their progress later in the semester. Discovering and addressing issues is critical to writing center work. This naturalized behavior becomes action research when a deliberate and systematic approach to collecting and analyzing data on the problem is employed and when, collaboratively and reflexively, the team enacts change.

What Is Action Research?

Action research was first employed by sociologist Kurt Lewin in the mid-1940s as an approach for systematically addressing broad social problems such confronting racial tensions and discrimination. Lewin wanted action research to address the chasm between social action and social theory, between practitioners and researchers, theory and practical problems (Dickens and Watkins 128). Action research is seen as an "everyday" type of inquiry for "ordinary" people. Ernest Stringer, for example, says it is "a systematic approach to investigation that enables people to find effective solutions to problems they confront in their everyday lives" (1). The idea and the method has also been widely used in various academic fields in the ensuing decades since Lewin's introduction, most prominently in educational research. Within English Studies, action research is an established approach within technical and professional writing—especially with community literacy based projects (e.g., Grabill; Faber; Blythe, et al.)—and within TESOL (Teaching English as a Second Language) (e.g., Burns).

Today, the term action research has quite a bit of elasticity— stretched to mean a variety of different approaches. Action research theorists Linda Dickens and Karen Watkins admit, "There is, in fact, no definitive approach to action research" (127). For preciseness, it has become popular to add an adjective to further distinguish a particular type of action research such as *participatory* action research (Godbee and Ozias), *schoolwide* action research (Calhoun), *teacher* action research (Dickens and Watkins), *organizational* action research (Dickens and Watkins), or *critical* action research (Blythe, et al.). Each of these is an attempt to call attention to particularly important aspects of different breeds of action research such as the involvement of community partners or to designate particular sites for research.

Since action research can mean so many things, I want to be clear how I'm using the concept in this chapter, and thus, what kind of action research I'm advocating for writing center researchers. I define action research as *collaborative, site-based, primarily qualitative research that involves the systematic collection of data to make responsible, collective decisions about enacting change in the researchers' own context.* Action research defined in this way shares similarities with how Jeffrey Grabill defines participatory action research which "demands the co-definition of problems, the cogeneration of knowledge, and collaborative action. It is concerned with local or community-based action, it is participatory, and it seeks to solve problems as articulated by those most in need" (148). Let's break down this definition into what I think are the essential qualities for writing center action research:

Collaborative

Action research, as I've defined it, is a team sport. Action research orientation flips the "normal" research approach where one researcher studies a larger group or phenomenon. Here, the group decides to collectively look for answers to a collective problem. One tutor might struggle with helping students with dissertations, another might skip all staff meetings. Those "problems" would probably not have sufficient scope for action research. However, if most tutors feel uncomfortable tutoring graduate students or if many of the tutors refuse to participate in ongoing staff development, those issues might be a starting point for action research. Ideally, the collective will identify the problem and will be in consensus about the need for research.

Writing center researchers who impose themselves upon their colleagues—"I have to do a research project for my class, and I've decided I'm going to solve the issue we have with advertising"—are likely to meet resistance or even hostility. The best way to begin an action research project is to listen to your colleagues. Should several staff meetings or several postings to a group discussion board circle back to the same problem time and time again, then a researcher could ask if the collective is interested in a more systematic inquiry. Even then, sometimes the answer is no (or just silence). Michael Grady writes in *Qualitative and Action Research* that "educators who take up action research run a risk of discovering things about their own practice that are negative, deficient, or limiting" (47). For this reason, systematic inquiry and the change that comes with action research can be intimidating.

Conversely, the collaborative nature of action research can make it even more rewarding than an individual research project because of the transformation the group can experience together. Emily Calhoun suggests that "a simple but essential component of school renewal may be individual and collective self-renewal: an orientation to work that means we are wiling to accept the discomfort and joy of never graduating from our study of teaching" (Calhoun 4). Though she is writing about school teachers conducting action research, the same applies to writing center professionals: if we want to continue to grow as practitioners, we need to continue to study what we are doing even if it is uncomfortable. Another benefit to collaborative research is the increased likelihood for sustainability of the change or "action." In projects where a lone researcher proposes or imposes a change to a community practice, it might be difficult for the collective to change and for the change to last beyond the researcher's time in the culture. When an action research project is taken on by the community, the community agrees to change and to continually reassess their practices.

Based in Own Context

The setting for an action research project is the researchers' own community or context. For writing center researchers, this means that an action research project would likely take place in a writing center or within a community in which the writing center is involved. That action research is conducted in our own communities only makes sense. It would be inappropriate to do a case study of writing center tutorials, say, at another center and then enact change at my own center, since the other centers might not have the same issues. The idea is that the problems will be identified and unique, contextual solutions will be enacted.

In this way, action research is closely related to **teacher research**—in fact, sometimes the terms are used interchangeably. Teacher research is where the teacher studies his or her own teaching practices. Yet action and teacher research differ in two important ways. First, although teacher research might be action-oriented, it does not have to be. Teacher researchers can use any methods of qualitative or quantitative inquiry to paint a descriptive picture of the their own classrooms. Teacher researchers do not have to enact change. Second, teacher research can be done individually. Action research, as I'm using the term here, must enact change and the decision to enact the change (and ideally the collection and analysis of data, too) must be made collaboratively by the members of the community being researched. One of the few writing center studies to call itself "action research," Cathy Hutchings' "Reaching Students: Lessons from a Writing Centre," actually would fall under what I'm calling teacher research. Hutchings' study is a qualitative analysis of end-of-session reports at her own center, but the study is neither enacted collaboratively nor does she enact change as part of the study.

Research played out in the researchers' own context on the researchers' own practices, the so-called "backyard research," is not easy and not without critics. The longer we are in a space or a community, we are conditioned to un-see many things. Humans cannot sustain a level of always-on sensory attention. We may unconsciously stop noticing things that are "normal"—things that happen repeatedly, things that are expected. Yet in qualitative research, the very things we have learned to un-see, that we have stopped noticing, are what we need to pay attention to as researchers. Because of this, it is infinitely easier to research a site that isn't "normal" to us. That is not to say there are not advantages to researching in your own communities or your own practices. It is almost always easier to gain access to and find willing participants when the participants know you already. In action research, if the collective is to agree to undertake a research project, they do so when they can see that they will benefit from the project. In terms of writing centers, action research projects that seek to improve the practice of tutoring, administrating, training, or other writing center initiatives will be most likely to appeal to the collective.

Planned, (Primarily) Qualitative Data Collection

Much of this book has focused on qualitative research because of its widespread use in Rhetoric and Composition. Though action research can draw on both qualitative and quantitative data, its orientation is better aligned with qualitative research methods, especially in an educational setting where complex, social interactions occur every hour on the hour. Though certain quantitative data—numbers—might alert a research team to an issue, the numbers alone do not tell the research team how to act. Action researchers must collect qualitative data such as observations, reflections, interviews, and artifacts and let analysis of that data point determine the change to enact.

Enacting Collective Change

Perhaps the defining characteristic of action research of any kind is its emphasis on change or action. Action research has to make a difference. As Ernest Stringer writes in *Action Research*, "If an action research project does not make a difference, in a specific way, for practitioners and/or their clients, then it has failed to achieve its objective" (12). A study can certainly be the first three of these: qualitative, collaborative, and conducted at the researcher's own site without being an action research project. Action research specifically aims to solve concrete issues such as how the writing center addresses student demand for services, how we make online tutoring more effective for students, or how we encourage professional development of staff.

Note here again that the change must be collective. In the sort of action research that I'm advocating, collaboration is key from start to finish. Colleagues decide together to research their practice. Together, they analyze their data, and together they enact change. This leads to the best chance that the action plan will be agreeable to those involved and sustainable for the long term.

What Is the Process for Action Research?

Schoolwide action research is a fancy way of saying, 'Let's study what's happening at our school, decide if we can make it a better place by changing what and how we teach and how we relate to students and the community; study the effects; and then begin again.'

—Emily Calhoun

Many qualitative research projects follow the research process discussed in *Part I*. Researchers identify a problem, review related literature, plan the study, collect data, analyze data, and report findings. Ernest Stringer says the basic action research routine is to look, think, and act. In other words, action researchers study the issue by collecting data (looking), imagine possibilities by scouring the data (thinking), and then put into place an action to resolve or alleviate the issue (acting). Thus, action research ends differently. Most qualitative research ends with reporting the findings. In action research, as I've noted, the process includes action, and, when enacted responsibly, it necessitates further research and reflection. A researcher engaged in action research might embark on a research process that look like this:

1. Identify a research problem collectively

2. Review related literature collectively

3. Plan for the collection and analysis of data; decide on role for group members

4. Collect data; share data among the group

5. Analyze data; share analysis with the group

6. Reflect on findings; brainstorm possible solutions; decide on roles for group members to put idea into action

7. Repeat steps 3–6, as needed.

8. Report findings to others.

The emphasis is on collaboration throughout the process, the process is recursive (it loops back instead of moving straight through), and there is potentially less emphasis on reporting findings to others. Those for whom the research is most important should be involved in the research process. Of course, reporting the data to others might very well be necessary because of course assignments, graduate school requirements, or the demands of the profession, and even though the research problem and solution are site-specific, it is likely that others may have similar issues and gain perspective from reading or hearing an action research report summary.

Calhoun suggests that several tangible conditions need to be established prior to beginning an action research project:

1. a faculty that seeks a better education for its students,

2. a public agreement about how collective decisions are made,

3. a facilitation team willing to lead the action research process,

4. study groups or liaison groups that meet regularly,

5. awareness and understanding of the action research cycle, and

6. technical assistance. (25–34)

Of course, these conditions contrast with other types of studies where a lone researcher can forge ahead without doing any of this groundwork.

In many cases, the **research problem** will already be identified by the members of the community and the research process is carried out to gather specifics about the problem. For instance, a center might sense that students or tutors are unhappy with their online tutoring sessions. (This might be found in student satisfaction surveys—a quantitative data point—where students routinely rate online sessions lower than face-to-face.) The center wants to improve their online tutoring and an action research study might be created to systematically gather data. By analyzing the data collectively, they then can decide on an action to address the problem or some part of the problem. Importantly, Andrew Johnson reminds action researchers that they may begin with an identified problem, but they should not start with an answer (14). The answer—the action that will be enacted—should come from the data (this is called an **inductive approach**).

Calhoun insists that action research teams "structure routines for continuous confrontation with data" (1) to make the best decisions for action. In other words, research teams should ask themselves: "knowing what we know now, should we act differently?" (Calhoun 89). If the answer is yes, action researchers make a change and continue to collect data systematically to evaluate and re-evaluate the change. If the action did not have the effect they thought it would, the team can reassess and take alternative actions.

For example, one year while I was directing a writing center, some of the native-English speaking tutors voiced their anxiety with tutoring non-native speakers. Working with some researchers with linguistics and TESOL backgrounds, we began to collect recordings of sessions and session logs, and the researchers also conducted interviews with tutors. Once all of the data was analyzed by the research team, the researchers suggested the anxiety might be, in part, from some of the tutors' unfamiliarity with rules of English. The researchers drafted a flow chart that tutors could use to decide how to respond to student errors. The action, in this case, was for tutors to change how they addressed errors. However, the flow chart was a bit too complicated to internalize (and tutors did not want it out on the table during a session), so the tutors' actions did not change nor did their anxiety about working with non-native students.

Though this project was somewhat action research oriented—the writing center team identified a problem and helped collect data—the writing center team did not get to be in on the conversations about data analysis or solutions. As a result, the perfectly rational solution proposed by the outside researchers, turned out not to work in the writing center context. Nonetheless, even when the community is in-

volved in every step (planning, collecting, analysis, and solution proposal), the change enacted might not work. The team will have to go
back to the data—or decide they need more or different data—and
think through different options. It is an ongoing process.

METHODS

Unlike the other chapters in Part II that have introduced different
methods for the collection and analysis of data, action research is not
a specific method but rather an approach to research that can draw on
any of the methods discussed in previous chapters, such as discourse
analysis, interviews, or fieldwork. Jeffrey Grabill describes action research as "fundamentally a *philosophical position* about how research
should be done" (147, emphasis added). Thus, readers wanting to take
on an action research project will want to return to previous chapters
here in Part II for discussions of available methods.

Action research teams who have consensus on a research issue to
study might turn next to discussions of what data is available and what
data needs to be collected. Common data collected for action research
include the following:

- studying texts/artifacts: writing samples, student products/per-
formances, websites, class journals, emails, letters
- studying individuals: conferences, interviews, rating checklists, diaries, logs, life/career histories, metaphor development
- studying talk: audio and video recordings of sessions, workshops, classes, meetings
- studying groups: questionnaires, focus groups
- studying tools: observation of software or peripherals use;
computer, tablet, phone, or pen and paper use by writers; reference materials use
- studying sites: thick description, field notes, research journals,
checklists, video and audio recording, data retrieval charts,
logs, T-charts, photographs, maps, layouts
- other possibilities: test scores, art (drawings, sketches, photos,
poems, short stories, etc.), archival data

As mentioned earlier, though action research may collect some quantitative data, researchers should primarily collect qualitative data

(Johnson; Burns; Stringer). Action researchers will want to draft plans for systematic data collection, storage, and organization. It is common that not all members of a research team have equal backgrounds in research, so those who have more experience should share their experiences and share readings with the collective so that careful research practices are maintained.

Limitations and Ethical Challenges

Since action research uses the methods described in previous chapters, the research limitations will be the same. For example, if the action research team selects a case study approach, the data will not be generalizable. Still, there are a few limitations to underscore here. The first is the issue of researchers researching their own communities. Since history favors objectivity in research, many are suspicious of a researcher's ability to be objective when focusing his or her gaze inward. For this reason, graduate students in Rhetoric and Composition are often cautioned about undertaking teacher research for thesis or dissertations. Frankly, it is difficult to pay attention as a researcher needs to do in your own setting, but here is where the research team helps. When everyone is systematically collecting and sharing the data, no one perspective can dominate.

In addition, there is not much precedent for action research in Rhetoric and Composition or writing center research, so it might be unfamiliar to others whom you want to collaborate with or in your audience. Finally, action research as defined here will almost always take longer than doing a study alone. Action researchers have to build consensus and momentum for the entire team.

Action researchers will also meet resistance to having their "issues" up for discussion by their colleagues. A few years ago, I was contacted by a local company who wanted to hire me to help their employees write better. The manager suggested I offer a few workshops because "good communicate was key" to their operations. We exchanged several emails as I tried to see what he thought the problem was. When I suggested, perhaps too brazenly, that workshops and tutorials were a good start, but that a little research might reveal other systemic ways to support improved communication at their company, the conversation abruptly ended. I suspect the manager did not want to believe the employees needed more than a lesson or two to stop making errors in their written reports and that the last thing he wanted was a nosy, university researcher poking around and suggesting changes to normal operating procedures.

It is important to remember, always, that being "studied" is not necessarily an enjoyable position for anyone. The participants in your study can feel judged—you might suggest how they could do things better or might suggest that they have particular blind spots. Though action research gives agency to the participants, the people being studied are also the ones doing the studying, it does not make the intimidation factor subside. In fact, in ways it might amplify it. If a graduate student observes a few of my tutoring sessions, for example, my writing center colleagues do not necessarily have to know about what he discovers. In an action research study, though, all of my colleagues would know. Action research makes people vulnerable. Writing center researchers engaging in action research need to always keep in mind the social and emotional difficulty of colleagues remaining open to the process. Further, *we* have to remain open: "many of us want others to change: students, colleagues, principals, district office personnel, parents, the world. In the early stages of school renewal, we are far less clear that we are actually asking ourselves to change" (Calhoun 4).

Despite these limitations, action research can achieve what other research approaches might not: a more unified community. Terrance Carson and Dennis Sumara's collection *Action Research as a Living Practice* shows how action research is relational. As they write in the introduction, "[A]ction research practices . . . are *particular* practices that require one's lived experiences be configured in particular ways. This does not only include one's beliefs, one's philosophies, one's attitudes to and about what constitutes research practices but, as well, includes the specific relational organization of one's living conditions" (xvi). Dickens and Watkins go so far as to say the two goals of action research are to improve and to involve (131), and Stringer says that "community-based action research results not only in a collective vision but also in a sense of community" (Stringer 11). Most writing centers want to foster just that.

Summary of Key Points: Action Research

- Action research gives teams a process and then pertinent data to make responsible changes.
- Action research should not be imposed upon a group; it should come out of group needs.
- Action research only works if teams begin with a question, not an answer.

For Discussion, Reflection, and Action

1. Who forms the community for your action research project? Who would the study mean the most to? Tutors in your center? Students in your center? Brainstorm a list of those who should be a part of an action research study in your community.

2. Action research is often focused on improving practice or lived realities for communities. What are areas in need of improved practice or lived realities in your community?

Recommended Resources

Stringer, Ernest. *Action Research.* 3rd ed. Los Angeles, CA: Sage, 2007. Print.

Johnson, Andrew. *A Short Guide to Action Research.* 3rd ed. New York: Addison Wesley, 2007. Print.

Research Notebook #2: Collecting Data

Nikki Caswell, Rebecca Jackson, and
Jackie Grutsch McKinney

Our plan when we began our collaborative longitudinal study of new writing center directors was to interview each of our nine participants monthly throughout the academic year. We intended to record each of the interviews, transcribe each interview, and then discard the recordings. Many of the interviews were conducted through Skype (video phone call) and were recorded with Quicktime screen recording. Others were conducted by phone and recorded with an audio recorder. One participant was interviewed only by email and the emails served as the research transcript.

We had a set of interview questions that we loosely followed each month for each participant that we called our interview guide. These questions asked the participants to think about the work they've done in the past month, what has occupied their time, what goals they have for the short- and long-term, what significant moments they've had, what stories they tell about their work, and what emotions they experience. The first month we asked a few additional questions about their background and their positions. Our interview plan was ambitious and things went according to plan, for the most part. However, there were several unexpected events that had us revising our plans on the fly.

First, we realized that interviewing each participant each month was a good goal, but not how it would play out exactly. Participants (and, occasionally, researchers) traveled, got sick, and got overwhelmed with work and/or personal lives. So, we did as best we could to stay in contact with participants. Instead of nine interviews from each of the nine participants, we had on average four to six interviews from each participant spaced throughout the year.

Second, we had a participant in our first round of interviews tell us that she'd be leaving her post as writing center director at the end of the semester. We considered briefly replacing her with someone else who would be in their post for the entire study. However, we thought it might be more representative of the status of writing center directors to include rather than exclude this participant. In our understanding, there is high turnover among writing center directors.

Our third unexpected event was an equipment failure; several of our interview sessions did not record. Luckily, we took notes during our interviews and, luckily, we did not lose an entire set of interviews from any one participant. We considered adding more interviews the following term so we'd have a similar number from each participant, but we didn't think that was necessary as we weren't doing any quantitative analysis in which having more transcripts from some participants would affect our findings. Furthermore, we were afraid that more data would change our scope: we wanted to interview new directors and, if we continued on, some participants might be in their third year. So we decided to make the most of what we had and to use informant checks to help us with any ambiguous data discoveries.

The final (yet not entirely unexpected) event was how much we connected with our participants. We found ourselves looking forward to our interviews and seeing how their roles evolved over the course of the year. Participants told us that they, too, found the conversations useful to process what was happening in their work; one called it free therapy. Now months after data collection has ended, we find ourselves wondering how they are doing and how issues we discussed throughout their first years were resolved. Several final interviews ended with promises of meeting up at conferences or staying in touch. Moreover, as a research team we've grown closer—more involved in one another's personal and professional successes and tragedies. This study, then, has fomented relationships—not a desired outcome at the start but certainly a welcome one.

Part III

8 Analyzing and Interpreting Your Data

If you're like most researchers, you might have worried during your data collection that you wouldn't find enough stuff for your study. However, by the end, that worry has likely transformed; now you might look at the huge pile of data you've accumulated and worry that you won't be able to use all of it. There's too much. If you have arrived at this particular point of crisis, good. You have made it to the final stage of researching when you move from what you've collected to figuring out what it means (the focus of this chapter) and how you'll share that with others (the focus of the final chapter).

Robert Stake reminds us that qualitative research—and most of the strategies explored in this book are qualitative—is also called interpretive research since "human behavior needs interpretation minute by minute" (36). Human behavior does not just "mean" something; we bring meaning or interpretation to it. This chapter will discusses two of the key elements of any study: analysis and interpretation. In some sources, analysis and interpretation are used synonymously, but I prefer how others, like Margaret LeCompte and Jean Schensul, make a clear distinction between the two because each identifies distinct steps that need to be taken in your study. **Analysis** is the process of sorting, summarizing, or condensing your data and **interpretation** is the process of critically reading your analyzed data to explain what it means to you as researcher (13–16).

Let's consider a simple example. Suppose you want to survey the tutoring staff at your local writing center to see what they think about your online tutoring interface. You design a five question online survey that asks them to rate particular aspects of the technology on a scale from one to five. If twenty-five tutors complete your survey, you'll have twenty-five completed survey instruments or 125 completed questions. If this were a paper survey, you would probably instinctively begin to tally your data by question. For question one, you'd see how many tutors rated the technology a one, a two, and so forth. Likely, an online survey program will do this type of analysis (or data sorting) for you by making summary tables or charts about how many and what percentage respondents answered each question each way. Once the data is sorted and condensed in this way, an interpretation is easier. I can notice where there are overwhelming majorities and where response is more divided. I can interpret and report trends; I can say what the trends are and what I think they mean. If most tutors rate a technology highly, I can interpret this as a high level of satisfaction.

Though it seems utterly reasonable to sort like questions with like questions and like responses with like responses, when we do this, we are making a choice of how to analyze our data. We could, instead, sort answers by respondent; we could see how many 5s, 4s, and so on each respondent gave. Or, we could group the questions to analyze them together. We could find probably any number of other ways to sort that simple survey data, each of which would shape how we read or interpret the data. The point is that there isn't one right way to do analysis or to form interpretations; you will need to be able to defend the choices you have made in your research report. Thus, this chapter will discuss strategies for analyzing and interpreting data so you can decide which methods are appropriate for your type of study and particular research questions.

QUALITATIVE ANALYSIS AND INTERPRETATION

Although this chapter appears in Part III and analysis and interpretation is indeed often considered a third stage of the research process, beginning analysis and interpretation of your data should happen concurrently with collection of data for your own sanity and for the quality of your research project. You will be better able to handle the data avalanche if you think about how to organize, sort, and save the data while the study progresses. This can be as simple as saving all related files to the same folder and devising a naming strategy so you can tell at a glance what each file contains. Or, it might mean subdividing the folder into files related to particular participants or by data points (interviews, artifacts, etc.).

Empirical research is fascinating because you are the first and only one to collect the particular data you've set out to collect, but that is also the reason that storing data can be nerve-wracking. If you lose it, no one is going to have a back up for you. Thus, make a plan for storing files in at least two ways (on your computer, on a portable drive, on the cloud, or even in hardcopy). Remember that you indicated how you would store data in your IRB application; make sure you refer back to how you said you'd save data there so you do not violate your own protocol. In the collaborative project described in the Researcher's Notebook, we each saved all project files on our personal computers and in Google Drive. We set up folders for transcriptions by participant, and we crafted a master data list to keep track of all project data.

Beyond just sorting and saving data, you can begin interpretation before data collection is complete. Blakeslee and Fleicher note a couple of different ways you can begin to do interpretation while collecting data: fieldnote summaries and research memos (165). Fieldnote summaries are when the researcher reads back through his or her notes after leaving the field and adds anything that he or she missed during the visit. In addition, the researcher would take a moment to reflect on particularly meaningful exchanges or events that he or she witnessed and jot these down. Research memos are similar but apply to all data points. After a first round of interviews, the first read of a corpus, or the observation of a few faculty workshops, say, the researcher takes some time to write a memo to him or herself reflecting on the data collected so far and making some notes about how future data collection might unfold. The researcher would note anything that seems to be surfacing as important in the data. Research (or analytic) memos are a key component of a grounded theory approach, described later in this chapter.

Another way to begin analysis during the data collection is to **transcribe** any audio- or video-recorded data as soon as possible after recorded. Transcription is the typing out of the word-by-word talk that you recorded. Before you do a transcription, it seems pretty straightforward. "I'll just type out what I hear," you might think. However, as Barbara Johnstone writes, "There are almost as many ways to transcribe speech as there are researchers who do so" (21). Researchers have a lot of decisions to make about how to transcribe and what gets transcribed. For instance, you'll need to decide if you'll include filler words (eh, ah, er), pauses, or outside noises in the transcript, and you'll have to decide how those will or won't be indicated in the transcript. Further, you'll learn quickly, that transcripts take a lot of time to complete. In my experience, an hour-long interview takes about six to eight hours to transcribe. All of this might make you want to pay someone else to do your transcriptions, which is considered perfectly ethical research behavior so long as you had indicated in that in your research proposal and in your informed consent to participants. However, you won't stay as closely connected to your data if someone else does your transcriptions. There are many judgment calls that you have to make when making a transcript, so you'll need to decide if you're willing to have someone else make those decisions for you. Either way, transcribing or reading transcripts along the way is a way to organize and prepare your data for interpretation. (For more on crafting transcripts, see Appendix D.)

Keeping track of your data, making it secure and organized, transcribing, and rereading your collected data keeps you in close contact with your data. All of this beginning analysis and interpretation allows you to focus on your study during the course of the data collection, so if something intriguing comes up in the first round interviews, you could follow up on that in your next round of interviews. Alternatively, you could adjust your protocol if you aren't seeing the sort of data that you need to answer your research questions. Therefore, I'd encourage you to plan to read, think, and write about your data as you collect it.

There will come a point when you reach the end of the time you planned for data collection. It is then that you will begin more strategic analysis and deeper interpretations. Nearly every source on conducting qualitative research will tell you that you need to read your data for patterns, group patterns into categories, and that from those categories, you will be able to answer your research questions. Though this is an apt summation of analysis and interpretation, I like the specific framework Carl Auerbach and Louise Silverstein provide in *Qualitative Data: An Introduction to Coding and Analysis,* which plots out six basic stages for how researchers move from "raw data" to "theoretical narratives," as well as Johnny Saldana's approach in *The Coding Manual for Qualitative Researchers.* I've borrowed from their approaches to present a possible writing center research approach to coding below.

Note that there are dozens—if not hundreds—of approaches to coding and qualitative analysis; the approach outlined here will get you started, but you will likely want to consult one or more of the coding resources at the end of the chapter for other approaches.

Stage One: Format and Read "Raw" Data

At the end of your data collecting, you will have (mostly) raw data— that is, data that has not yet been fully analyzed or interpreted.[25] Your goal in this stage is to finish organizing all of your files, transcribing as needed, and to read every bit of data at least twice. You'll also want to put all of your data into a similar format in preparation for the next stages. Some people simply print everything in hard copy and organize it in a binder. Others put the files into a CAQDAS (Compuer-Assisted Qualitative Data Analysis Software) program (e.g., NVivo, Atlas.ti, Weft QDA, Dedoose, and HyperRESEARCH). These programs differ in particular functions but generally allow users to upload files and make coding and sorting across various files easy. Other researchers will chunk data into a spreadsheet or table leaving a column (or more) blank on the right for coding. I like using hardcopies to begin the coding process, though I find CAQDAS programs more useful once I have developed my coding scheme.

Stage Two: Isolate Relevant Data for Coding

Your next step will be a step toward reduction of data, moving from all of the data to isolating what data is most relevant to your research questions. To discern this, you'll need to read your research questions again and remind yourself what you wanted to find out at the outset. Then, figure out which data will allow you to answer your question in the timeframe you have. Researchers *can* use all of the data collected (this is called comprehensive sampling) or sample within the data set (much the same as sampling for participants as described in Chapter 5). Depending on the project goal, researchers may use convenience sampling by selecting readily available texts, criterion sampling by selecting only texts that have a certain criteria, or random sampling within data sets (Blythe 207–8). Likely, you'll find that one data point is less helpful than you thought it might be or that you won't be able to adequately report on all of data given the size of your report. When that happens, you can put some data aside. (Note that I didn't say delete it! You might want to return to it.) Though I believe a degree of data reduction occurs in every qualitative study, it is probably something you want to talk through with someone else who has experience with your topic or research method. Sometimes there's data that seems to not "fit" with the rest initially, but after talking it through with someone else you might realize that if you reconsider some of your beginning assumptions, that data is absolutely necessary for the study.

Stage Three: Find Repeating Ideas/First Pass Coding

When you have your data files formatted for review and when you've decided what data to use, you will then begin the actual coding process. A **code**, according to Saldana, is "most often a word or short phrase that symbolically assigns a summative, salient, essence-capturing, and/or evocative attribute for a portion of language-based or visual data" (3). In simplest terms, a code is a label that you assign to a piece of your data. In most research in writing center studies, codes are developed out of the data and not *a priori* of data collection. This means that you don't go to your data with a set of labels to apply to the data. Instead, as you read you create your own **emergent codes** by labeling the data in a way that, as Saldana suggests, is summative, salient, essence-capturing, or evocative. Codes are typically short; most codes are one to three words.

Before you start to label your data, you will want to define a **unit of analysis** that works for your project.[26] Units of analysis refers to the size of each chunk or piece of data that you will code. Various types of units of analysis are used in Rhetoric and Composition—anything from words, to phrases, to conversational exchanges, to paragraphs, to entire documents. The size of your unit of analysis will depend both on your research question and on the types of data you collected. If you are doing discourse analysis of a set of tutor training texts and wonder about how readers are addressed, your unit of analysis might be each phrase or sentence. This type of unit that can be discerned by punctuation or grammatical rules is a **syntactic unit** (Grant-Davie 275). If, however, you have collected tutoring transcripts, your unit of analysis might be each talk turn. That type of unit is called a **functional unit** (Grant-Davie 275); the length of this unit is determined by the speaker or writer, not by syntax. Other functional units might include breaking the text each time a new topic is introduced by a speaker or when a change of activity happens as indicated in your fieldnotes. As a general rule, you keep your unit of analysis consistent throughout your data; that means if your unit of analysis for one data point is entire documents, you would not code another data point sentence by sentence.

As you read your data this time, try labeling each unit of analysis. In first pass coding, you can just assign codes as they come to you. In a way, this process is similar to the familiar tutoring process where a tutor asks a writer to say what a paragraph is doing in one or two words to address orders of organization and coherence. Ask yourself: what's happening in this data as related to my research question? First pass coding might include manifest, in vivo, or latent coding. **Manifest codes** are labels for observable phenomena (Blythe 217); that is, manifest codes are for things which are visible with no (or very minimal) interpretation needed. For example, if I am coding a set of writing center web pages, I might be interested in colors used in creating sites, so I code by color. When I see blue, I would code *blue*. Any researcher would, in theory at least, code these the same way. In contrast to manifest codes are **latent codes**, for which the researcher infers or makes a judgment to code. For instance, I might be interested in the tone of writing center websites, so I might see some phrases which I decide to label as *friendly*. The actual language used on the site might not say the word *friendly*, but I have inferred that the authors of the site are trying to create that feeling with their words or other content. However, if the code you assign are the participant's (or in the document's) wording, then the codes are **in vivo codes** and you typically write the code in quotation marks. For example, if a writing center site says, "we offer a friendly, welcoming place to talk about your writing," I could code this with an in vivo code of *"friendly"* to remind ourselves that the code comes from the participant or document itself. Most, but not all, Rhetoric and Composition projects use latent coding and/or in vivo coding more than manifest coding.

Stage Four: Code Themes/Second Pass Coding

When you do first pass coding, you might end up with many, many codes. One of my PhD students ended up with over one hundred after a first pass of her data. As you might suspect, this is too many codes to work with. In second pass coding, you narrow your focus to codes which might be surfacing as frequent or compelling and you think

about whether any of your codes might be combined. This stage further condenses your data but also is important because, as Elizabeth
Chiseri-Strater and Bonnie Sunstein note, "in qualitative research,
no single piece of data stands alone by itself as evidence" (141). One
line from one transcript or from one artifact is not enough to call
it representative of the population or site under consideration. This
makes sense if we consider an example. Suppose my research question
involves finding out tutor perceptions of graduate student writers. If
one tutor in one interview says one time that graduate students are her
"favorite," it would be irresponsible for me to report that tutors in the
study favor graduate student writers. So, we look for patterns to help
tell us what we can say responsibly.[27] Note that it is much more difficult to find relevant, repeating patterns if our data set is too small.
Interviewing participants more than once and gathering multiple data
points can help you to justify your findings better. This idea of finding
similar or identical idea/terms within your data is called **triangulation**. Though, the term implies that you need to find three instances,
you actually just need to find more than one (the more the better,
however). If you are doing a case study, you might look for repeating
ideas within the data from each participant individually, whereas if
you are doing an ethnography, you will look across the participants or
with discourse analysis across the corpus.

As you decide which codes to focus on, look at how frequent a code
appears and how compelling a code is. There is no magic number of
codes to reduce to in this stage, but working with more than twenty
to thirty codes will probably prove difficult to track for you as a researcher and for potential readers of your research. Keep in mind that
this again might be a stage where you set aside some data for another
project. That is, perhaps, like my student who had 100 codes, you find
many of them really compelling. That's great, but you can decide, like
she did, which codes to focus on for the first project to come from the
data. She can return to her data after her dissertation to revisit some of
the codes she had to set aside to finish her degree.

It is useful at this point to develop a **coding scheme**. A coding
scheme is a table that can guide your second pass coding and that
you'll eventually share with readers of your research. You'll have a horizontal row for each code and columns for (1) a description of the code,
(2) an example from your research data of something you labeled with
that code, and sometimes researchers include (3) a counter-example to

illustrate an example from the data that would not fit into the code. Then, you'll do the second pass coding where you use your coding scheme to go back to the data and recode each unit of analysis (if possible) with your short list of codes. It is always surprising what new things you see in the data when you do second pass coding—especially when you have a lot of data. It can also happen that second pass coding reveals the need to further cut or combine codes, and then to read the data again using your revised coding scheme.

Stage Five: Group Codes into Categories

In this stage, you look to see if codes can be grouped together in a way that suits the data. Say, for instance, you interviewed tutors about interactions with writers. At several points, tutors mentioned phone conversations or email threads with students, and you coded these themes in your data as "communication via phone" and "communication via email" respectively. However, at this stage, you might see a good reason to put these two codes together under the category of "non-face-to-face communication." There is no magic number of codes or categories researchers must end with. Researchers must consider which codes seem different manifestations of the same phenomena and which do not. It is not uncommon for researchers to think particular codes might fit together at one point and later decide those codes do not. Keep notes on how your coding and categorizing evolves.

Stage Six: Use Categories to Write Theoretical Narratives

Finally, we use our categories to shape theoretical narratives that address our research questions (Auerbach and Silverstein 40). In order to craft a narrative (a story) of the research, we have to consider what the data is telling us and what it means. Then, as Chiseri-Strater and Sunstein describe, "what finally emerges from our piles of data is not a contrived story but rather one that is verifiable and confirmable because it is always based on the vast amount of sharply focused material we've collected, sorted, interpreted, analyzed, and rendered accessible to a reader" (157). The stories we write simply show the reader how the codes and categories fall into relationships with one another and show how important particular codes or categories were for particular participants or artifacts.

At the end, we should be able to say "this is what I found" and "this is what I think it means." Both of these claims should be grounded in our data. We don't insist that our interpretation is singularly correct. Blakeslee and Flescher remind us that "there is no single correct meaning to be found in your data" (168). Others could come to the same data and make different interpretations, but so long as your interpretation is supported, it is valid and valuable.

Concerning Validity and Reliability

Two concerns of any study are whether it is reliable (a study will find the same results each time or throughout the course of the study) and whether it is valid (the study is appropriate for the research question). One way that qualitative researchers address these issues is through **informant checks**. Informant checks occur when researchers (who are using human subjects) either talk through their interpretations with participants or provide participants with a draft of their research report and ask participants to give feedback. In the case study project highlighted in the Research Notebook sections of this book, we also provided participants with transcripts so they could make any corrections or clarifications they felt necessary. During this process, a couple of participants also noted parts of the transcripts they wanted us to omit from the data set. Having an open relationship with participants like this makes the process less like gotcha journalism; we allowed participants to change their minds about what they told us or how they said something.

Another good research practice while doing coding is to have someone not involved in the research code a small set of your data to confirm whether another researcher would label the same units of analysis with the codes you have. (This would be more important with latent codes where the researcher has made inferences or judgments about codes.) This process is called **inter-rater reliability** and is used to some degree in writing center studies but only in larger projects. However, writing studies scholar Grant-Davie is skeptical about what inter-rater reliability actually does. He writes, "What reliability tests really do when they yield high rates of agreement is show that the researchers have successfully created a small, specialized community of readers who have been 'normed,' or trained to interpret the data in the same way" (283). He believes that inter-rater reliability tests obscure the fact that data is interpreted by the researcher, not described; that is, coding is subjective, and for Grant-Davie, that is perfectly okay. He stresses that "coding systems are no more objective than any other ways of reading, so we should not expect them to be purged of subjectivity" (285).

As an alternative, Stuart Blythe suggests that qualitative researchers must make their coding decisions visible to themselves as researchers through writing themselves research memos or making notes about coding decisions and writing about those decisions in their research reports. This method is one way of engaging in what James Porter and Patricia Sullivan call critical research; critical research keeps ethical research practices central not through outside confirmation necessarily but by prioritizing the researcher's commitment, respect, and care for participants (Blythe 234–35).

OTHER TYPES OF ANALYSIS AND INTERPRETATION

The general process provided above would work with most writing center projects with qualitative data; still, you'll likely see variations on this general approach or other approaches in some Rhetoric and Composition research that you read. Thus, I want to briefly mention other approaches of analysis which are possibilities for writing center researchers.

Quantitative Analysis

If your data includes numerical data, your analysis will likely contain some quantitative or statistical analysis. Richard Haswell has written that quantitative data can provide insight, transgression, challenge-ability, and persuasion to the work of composition studies and especially in distribution of research at a researcher's own institution (188). Though it is outside the scope of this book to provide detailed instruction on all possible statistical analyses, Haswell notes that most quantitative analyses within writing studies count and compare (187). Frequency counts (e.g., how often an answer is given to a survey question) are usually computed by the researcher or by the survey program itself.

Quantitative analysis becomes slightly more complicated at the level of comparison where a researcher looks at one variable in relationship to another variable. For example, a researcher might look at how a tutor answers a survey question in relationship to how an administrator (like a writing center director) does. Different statistical equations allow you to compare these relationships to say whether the difference is significant. **Significant** in quantitative research is a statistical term—not synonymous with simply "meaningful." It means that there is a mathematical difference discerned in the comparison. Those not familiar with statistical comparisons might parse the data themselves and see that tutors, gave a certain response forty-seven percent of the time and directors gave a response fifty-eight percent of the time. The difference may look large, but based on statistical analysis, the difference may or may not be significant.

There are many different statistical equations—t-test, ANOVA, Chi-Square, and so on—that researchers choose between based on the types of variables and data they have. John Cresswell provides a helpful table for deciding between eight different tests in *Research Design* (153). Mary Sue MacNealey discusses four of the most used tests in writing studies in *Strategies for Empirical Research in Writing* (104–8), and Cindy Johanek discusses the pitfalls of sloppy quantitative analysis in *Composing Research*. All of these sources will offer you an introduction to the types of comparison analysis you might wish to do, but Richard Haswell's advice about taking a course in statistics and/or working with someone who has expertise in statistical analysis will likely be most important to your success with quantitative analysis (194). (This advice is underscored by Karen Rowan in her After the Study piece.) Many universities, in fact, will have a person or office who can provide help with statistical analysis.

One caution worth mentioning here about quantitative data analysis and comparisons: correlation is not causation. If your analysis suggests a significant relationship between two categories, it does not mean that one causes the other. If analysis shows, for example, that students who identify as female attend the writing center more often, it does not mean that identifying as female *causes* those students to attend more often.

Grounded Theory

Grounded theory is an approach to research popularized by Bernie Glaser and Anselm Strauss in their book, *The Discovery of Grounded*

Theory published in 1967. Grounded theory is an approach to qualitative research and can be used with a variety of methods, though it is typically used for longitudinal studies involving interviewing and/or fieldwork. In the grounded theory approach, the researcher engages in analysis and data collection at the same time, employs the "constant comparative method," which requires making connections across data throughout the research process, uses memo-writing, and conducts the literature review after data collection (Charmaz 5–6). The idea behind grounded theory is that a researcher would not bring a theory as a lens to look at the data, but rather that a theory would emerge from the data—be *grounded* in the data. In grounded theory, there are three stages of coding: open coding, axial coding, and selective coding (Neff 135). Though Joyce Neff notes that few writing center research projects historically have used grounded theory (141), the popularity of grounded theory approaches in writing studies in general seems to be on the rise. Kathy Charmaz's *Constructing Grounded Theory* provides an update and slight departure from Glaser and Strauss's seminal work—an approach called constructivist grounded theory—and Neff explores how grounded theory might be used in writing center studies in her chapter "Capturing Complexity: Using Grounded Theory to Study Writing Centers."

Activity Theory

There is increasing interest in writing studies in activity theory and a number of interrelated theories (including WAGR analysis, distributed cognition, and actor-network theory) that are being used for shaping studies and reading data. Bill Hart-Davidson notes that these types of theories "can be understood within—rather than apart from—the sociohistorical conditions that humans inhabit" (157). Activity theory in particular, as described by Cheryl Geisler and Shaun Slattery, "is a conceptual system that conceives of human behavior as goal driven and mediated by artifacts" (188). The five basic principles are that 1) human behavior is goal-oriented; 2) human behavior is hierarchical; 3) human behavior is both external and internal—we do things in our mind and in the world; 4) human behavior is always mediated—we use symbolic and physical tools to do things; and 5) human behavior develops and changes as tools change (Geisler and Slattery 189–90). Thus, discerning the artifacts and tools that humans use and craft to reach goals is key for activity theory analysis. These tools and artifacts can be conceptual (for instance, the idea of higher-order concerns and lower-order concerns popular in writing centers can be seen as a conceptual tool used in tutoring) or material (perhaps the use a particular technology in writing center work). Many also think of written and speech genres as conceptual tools, so genre analysis is now closely intertwined with activity theory ideas; Charles Bazerman and David Russell's collection *Writing Selves/Writing Societies: Research from Activity Perspectives* offers good examples of genre analysis.

Narrative Analysis

Narrative analysis pays attention to stories told by participants orally or within the corpus of texts studied. According the Leslie Rebecca Bloom, narrative analysis has three essential tenets: 1) "it is concerned with using individual lives as the primary source of data"; 2) "it is concerned with using narratives of the 'self' as a locating from which the researcher can generate social critique and advocacy"; and 3) "it is concerned with deconstructing the 'self' as a humanist conception" (310). Essentially, researchers try to understand how identities are shaped by the stories of "selves" that participants share. For example, in "Sharing Our Stories: Using Narrative Inquiry to Examine Our Writing Centers," Lauren Schiely critically examines her personal stories about writing center work. Narrative analysis is not the telling of stories or the collecting of stories; narrative inquiry uses stories as data to examine what work stories do for the teller and how the story positions the teller within the cultures the teller operates.

FINAL THOUGHTS ON ANALYSIS AND INTERPRETATION

The evidence doesn't make it true. The evidence makes us confident that what we are thinking is right.

—Stake

Stake's words here should remind us that when we do analysis and interpretation, we are not proving something. We are making a reading that we support with evidence. Other readers, other interpretations could likely be made and supported by the same data. No matter. When we analyze and interpret our data, we present readers with our frames and processes for arriving at a conclusion we feel confident in making. How we present our findings convincingly is addressed in the next chapter.

For Discussion, Reflection, and Action

1. Record a tutoring session or other conversation and practice transcribing. Notice what challenges you have. What is difficult to transcribe? What is revealed to you in the process of transcribing? (Remember that more advice on transcribing can be found in Appendix D.)

2. Below is a brief excerpt from a transcript from the project described in the Research Notebook, which we found really compelling. Looking at this, try coding for both latent and manifest codes. Ask someone else to code the same passage and note how your codes overlap and diverge. Discuss the moments in the transcript that are most compelling for you.

    This situation, I didn't spend a lot of time working on it, but I'll tell you it is very important for peer tutors that we lead. We have writing center peer tutor training every Friday morning for about 45 minutes. In those sessions we try to cover as much as we can, but lately we've been focusing on APA documentation style since a lot of the professors on campus require their students to use that style. We want to make sure our tutors are proficient, and that at least they know where to go to help clients that come in. I just found out that one of our peer tutors has not been showing up regularly for our training, and I think that set a bad precedent for the rest of the students who were "well, she can get away with it; the rest of us can too."

    So, my assistant director who runs the training every Friday morning let me know that this student wasn't attending. I had them come to my office, you know, just let her know the importance of being here and being professional because our theme this year in the writing center is professionalism. If she had a problem, just come and let us know and see how we can solve that problem

*with her. But just to not show up and ignore the whole situation;
we're not going to tolerate that.*

*And I talked to her like a daughter; I have three grown daugh-
ters, so I was able to relate to her and share my experiences of
being a mother and how we need to be responsible. [inaudible]
you don't want to disobey the associate director. You don't want
to disobey her because you never know when you are going to need
her for references. You probably will some day; you will need her
for references when you graduate so you want to be able to do the
best you can as an employee. And as a student as well. She took
that very well from my standpoint. I wasn't really preaching to
her. I just wanted her to know the importance of her being here,
and that I expected her to be here for the rest of the training for
this year, this semester. [Isatta, November Interview]*

RECOMMENDED RESOURCES

Auerbach, Carl, and Louise Silverstein. *Qualitative Data: An Introduc-
tion to Coding and Analysis.* New York: New York UP, 2003. Print.
Blythe, Stuart. "Coding Digital Texts and Multimedia." *Digital Writ-
ing Research.* Ed. Heidi McKee and Danielle DeVoss. New York:
Hampton Press, 2007. Print.
Charmaz, Kathy. *Constructing Grounded Theory.* Thousand Oaks,
CA: Sage, 2006. Print.
Saldana, Johnny. *The Coding Manual for Qualitative Researchers.*
Thousand Oaks, CA: Sage, 2009. Print.

9 Sharing Your Research

After the long hours of preparing, compiling secondary research, recruiting participants, and surveying or observing or coding data, finally you arrive at the moment where you need to report what you've found. Reporting research can take several forms, and this chapter explores audiences, approaches, and genres for reporting writing center research. The idea with reporting research, particularly qualitative research, is to paint a vivid picture of your research. You'll want your audience to understand the choices you made in crafting the study, conducting the study, analyzing your findings, and presenting your conclusions. To do so requires that you start at the beginning and replay for them how you came to understand what you know now. Should you leave out any steps, your audience may be confused, doubtful, or annoyed.

TEXT-BASED AND MULTIMODAL PROJECTS

In many cases, you won't deliver your research report directly. Instead, you'll rely on a document to convey your findings to an audience. Writing center research is presented in text-based or multimodal reports in these forms:

Stakeholder Reports

Many writing centers will be asked to report semesterly or annually on their activities including assessment and research. Typically the audience for such reports directly influences the funding and support of the writing center. Thus, stakeholder reports can be high stakes.

Class Projects

Often writing center research is conducted for a course project—for both courses in which writing center studies is the main topic and for which it is not. In these cases, instructors will provide detailed assignment guidelines.

Theses and Dissertations

Most graduate programs require a major research project as the final step of a degree. (Some undergraduate programs also require a thesis for graduation.) Each university—and sometimes each department within a university—will have slightly different requirements for what these research reports look like. In my department, for example, undergraduate honors theses are typically about forty to fifty pages, masters theses are typically seventy-five to one hundred and fifty pages, and doctoral dissertations are twice as long as that (150–300 pages). Needless to say, other universities will have different expectations, so check with your advisor.

Poster Presentations

Poster presentations are an increasingly popular genre for writing studies research. Poster presentations are either paper posters or a digital text displayed on a screen. Often, at academic conferences, the author of the poster presentation is on hand during an assigned time to talk with readers about the poster/screen text.

Journal Articles, Webtexts, or Book Manuscripts

Writing center research often is written for publication in one of the three dedicated peer-reviewed journals for writing center studies: *The Writing Lab Newsletter, The Writing Center Journal,* and *Praxis: A Writing Center Journal.* Additionally, writing center research is also published in other writing studies journals such as *WPA: Writing Program Administration, Composition Studies, Kairos,* and *College Composition and Communication.* Each of these journals has different manuscript and submission requirements (posted on each's websites). Several publishers will also publish book-length writing studies research, including Utah State University Press, Southern Illinois University Press, Peter Lang, Routledge, Hampton Press, and Parlor Press.

Though there are different ways to present research findings, the traditional format for reporting (empirical) research is the IMRaD format, which stands for introduction, methods, results, and discussion. Using this format makes your research legible to other writing study researchers, allowing them to better use your research as a jumping off point for their own work. Moreover, this format is understood by researchers in other fields, which means there is a greater chance of your research making sense to others at your institution outside of writing studies and others. Though the thought of writing to a set format may seem rigid or formulaic, researchers who use it are still able to make their data and findings interesting and engaging.

The **introduction** section provides the reader the context for the research study, including an explanation of the research problem, a review of related literature, the theoretical frame, and an overview of the project or report. Many times in writing studies and writing center studies projects, the introduction and review of literature are two separate sections or chapters.

The **methods section** describes for the reader how the study was conducted; it should provide enough detail that another researcher could replicate your study. Importantly, the methods section must also say why the study was conducted as it was. It is necessary to make the case that, given your situation and limitations, you conducted the study in the best possible way to answer your research question. Readers should be convinced that there was no other plausible way.

The **results section** is also called the **findings section**. Here, you provide a summary of the data you collected in the course of your study to answer your research question. As discussed in Chapter 8, it's impossible to provide your readers with all of your data. So, in this section you focus on the data you have time and/or space to present in the genre you're using. If you are writing a dissertation or a book, you have more room, obviously, than with a poster presentation. Still, the tendency to try to report all of the findings and all of the data in one report is pressing. Yet it is hardly ever possible, especially with the sorts of qualitative research that most researchers in writing studies conduct. The results section will be in many cases as long or longer than all of the other sections combined, so you do have room to go in-depth into the themes you decide to use.

Your task in the final section, the **discussion section,** is threefold. First, you must tell your reader what to make of your findings. What is the takeaway? What are the implications? This is where you answer the always present question in writing: *so what?* Second, you need to connect your findings back to the bigger conversation. You'll return readers to the ideas you noted in the literature review and show how your answer to your research question(s) speak back to existing research. Finally, you will plot out what readers need to know next. Based on what you did find, now what should you or other researchers study next?

You'll note that the first two sections—the introduction and methods sections—were a part of your research proposal. Many times, a researcher can copy and paste large chunks from the proposal document into the report; however, you will need to adjust your text to account for any changes that you had to make to your proposed methods, to change the tense from future to past tense, and to add secondary sources into your lit review that will better prepare your readers for the patterns you discuss in your findings and discussion section. In Appendix C, I've included Driscoll and Perdue's RAD rubric, which is a wonderful tool for evaluating your own reports in IMRaD format. Furthermore, Susan Blau, John Hall, and Tracy Strauss's article "Exploring the Tutor/Client Conversation: A Linguistic Analysis" is an example of a writing center study in IMRaD format that would be a good model for those using IMRaD format for shorter reports. They begin with a section called "Background," which includes a statement of their research problem, a description of their theoretical lens (linguistic analysis), and methods. Then, they divide their findings into three sections relating to the most significant categories that emerge in their analysis: questions, echoing, and qualifiers. These sections include extended examples from their transcript data. Their conclusion section includes their discussion—saying what their findings mean to readers and pointing readers toward "future directions" (39).

Though the IMRaD format might be new to some readers of this book, many will likely have extensive experience with other types of research writing. Much of what you already know about engaging readers, being rhetorically savvy, and maintaining your authorial integrity applies to research writing, too. Based on my undergraduate and graduate students' work, I'll offer a few more suggestions which apply to writing center research reports in particular.

Leave It Messy

Research narratives that are too clean and tidy make readers suspicious. It is expected that your study has limitations—you simply don't have unlimited resources, time, and perfectly compliant research participants. Be upfront about what you were able to study and what didn't go according to your plan. Also, you will likely have complicated findings—as was discussed in the previous chapter. Do not oversimplify what you discovered. Sometimes the most interesting finding can be results that initially seem to contradict each other.

Use Subheadings

Scholars from some disciplinary backgrounds use subheadings frequently, but others do not. Subheadings in empirical research and in writing studies are common and expected.

Provide Enough Data So Readers Trust How You Came to Your Conclusions

I like to see in research reports actual data that was collected—and quite a bit of it. If you collected quantitative data, show me the numbers. If you collected qualitative data, you can't show me all of it, but show me enough quotations from transcripts, portions of texts, images, or whatever else that you collected so there is ample evidence of your claims. Sometimes, in addition to using data within the findings section, researchers will include more in the appendix, such as an interview transcript or responses to an open-ended question on a survey.

Use Multimodality to Add Dimension to Your Text

Aristotle famously instructed rhetors to discern "available means of persuasion" when constructing an argument, and that advice holds true today. When composing, we have many available means of communication even when writing a conventional genre, such as a thesis or journal article. In those situations, we can incorporate photographs, charts, tables, graphs, maps, and other visualizations along with the text to help readers understand our data and our theorizing about our data. In other types of reports, we might be able to incorporate audio, video, or animation as well. (Be sure not to use images, audio, or video of participants whom you said would remain confidential in your reporting.)

Beware of the Pedagogical Imperative

In the field of writing studies, there has long been a pressure (called by Karen Kopelson the "pedagogical imperative") to turn to pedagogical answers (teaching solutions) in your implication section, even when the study was unrelated to teaching. In writing center research, this equates to a turn toward tutoring. So, for instance, if I was doing the study I contemplated in Chapter 2 about writing center blog readership, I might feel compelled (or actually be compelled by journal reviewers or a dissertation committee) to say what my findings mean for tutoring. (The *so what?* question becomes *what does this mean for teaching/tutoring?*) The problem is that some studies are not about teaching or tutoring, so for those studies teaching and tutoring should not factor into the implications because you'd simply be guessing about the connection.

PRESENTATIONS

Many times researchers will present their research in addition to or instead of producing a written report. Presentations can bring out anxieties you did not even know you had because they require public speaking and typically have pretty high stakes; if you flub, it could mean getting a lower grade, looking foolish, or not getting a job. Or, that's how it feels. In reality, audiences are typically pretty understanding; in my experience, they rarely know or care how nervous I am. If I know my material and my research is interesting and carefully executed, the audience does not fixate on my minor speaking mistakes.

Still, presentations are difficult because time limits mean we need to be very selective about what we report. It is not uncommon, for example, for a panelist at a conference to only have fifteen to twenty minutes for presenting. With empirical research projects, this means making tough choices. We still need to give the audience some sense of the project, its relation to other research, our methods, and then report the analysis of our data, speculate on what our study means for the field, and suggest future directions for study. That's six objectives to meet and we might well have less than three minutes to speak to each one.

Writing center research is commonly presented orally in these situations:

Classroom Presentations

Instructors often ask students to present their findings to the class. In these situations, the assignment requirements can be your guide to length, goal, and format.

Oral Defenses of Theses or Dissertations

Many graduate programs have a major project for a graduation requirement. Often, graduate students have to present their findings orally and answer questions about their project as the final step of their degree. Sometimes these are open to the public and sometimes it is just the student and his or her committee members. Most defenses last one to two hours; students should ask how much of that time should be devoted to the oral presentation and how much time should be reserved for questions because this varies from school to school.

Conference Presentations

Writing center studies has one of the best networks of international, national, and regional (and even mini-regional and state) conference associations in higher education. Peer tutors and administrators in the US will easily find a nearby conference for presenting their research, or they can travel afar to join in academic discussions of writing center work and scholarship. (Take a look at the International Writing Center Association's website to find links to all of these writing center associations: www.writingcenters.org.) Furthermore, scholars are able to present at other conferences focused on writing studies, pedagogy, or peer learning. A conventional academic conference has concurrent sessions each with panels of presenters in different rooms presenting at the same time. Conference attendees can decide which panel to attend during each session. This means speakers cannot be sure how many (or how few!) audience members will be in attendance for their presentation. However, each conference—even the same association from year to year—is a bit different in conception and format.

Job Talks/Invited Lectures

For job seekers in academia—especially for faculty positions—the "job talk" is one part of the on-campus interview. The job talk is a presentation given on your research, typically for about forty-five minutes followed by fifteen minutes of questions. Sometimes, interviewees are asked to speak about their research agenda—what they've done and where they see their research headed. Other times, they are asked to present on one project. If you are applying for a writing center position, it is best to present writing center research.

Stakeholder Meetings

Writing center research is also of consequence to local settings and often writing center professionals are asked to present on the research to stakeholders: administrators, colleagues, staffs, faculty across the curriculum, advisory boards, benefactors, and even student governments.

When preparing for a presentation of any kind, you have to find out the specific rhetorical situation you will be in. Who is your audience? Can you get a list of names and titles? What's the purpose of the presentation? What format should it take? What limitations of time or technology must you work within? What is the context (material and historical) and setting for your presentation? Though the situation makes every situation unique, there are some general recommendations for reporting research orally.

Know Your Format

Many writing center conferences ask presenters to select from a variety of presentation formats, such as individual and panel presentations, roundtables, or workshops; the call for proposals should define the expectations for these different formats. Many writing center conferences require that presenters engage the audience by building in audience participation. Select whatever format best suits your content and then deliver in that format when presenting.

Stick to the Time Limit

No one is happy when speakers go over their time limit. In nearly every speaking situation, if a presentation goes long, it will disrupt the schedule. In the case of class or academic presentations, it might mean that the next speaker does not have enough time. It is possible that the moderator will ask you to stop speaking even if you have not finished. In my classes, for instance, I sometimes use a timer during my student presentations. When it goes off, they have to stop speaking as a way of learning to stick within time limits. Students who are not finished reveal that they haven't prepared well enough and are graded on the partial presentation. This replicates other situations, such as when the dean or provost might give you just ten minutes to make a pitch. Don't doubt that he or she (or an assistant) won't cut you off if you try to go over your time. They will.

Use Speaking Notes

Though many in English studies, particularly those in literature and linguistics, frequently read papers at academic conferences or job talks, this is less common in writing and writing center studies. Most in this field use notes to talk through their research—either on a screen or on paper—often accompanied by slides, handout, or other visual element. For presentations, I'm likely first to write out exactly what I want to say because I find that writing helps me work out nuances and transitions. Plus, it helps cement the argument into my memory. But during the presentation I have just an outline or a script with key passages highlighted in front of me that I glance at while I'm speaking. If I just rely on memory (no notes), I tend to leave out important pieces or get ahead of myself.

Use Visuals Strategically, Purposefully

Often, we're required or expected to have visual elements with our presentations. Even when this is the case, we ought to think carefully about what the visual will add to the presentation—what's its value? Visuals can illustrate complex ideas, can underscore main arguments, and can be a physical take-away the audience can consult later. Slideshow presentations that simply echo the exact same words the speaker is saying aren't a valuable element. Likewise, audience have become numb to slideshows that overly rely on bullet points to organize ideas.

Give Background Information

Many classical epic poems famously start *in medias res;* your presentation should not. Even in a situation when someone has requested a presentation of you—say a teacher or an administrator—you must get everyone at the starting gate with you before the gun goes off. As we research we spend so much time with our data that we imagine everyone is where we are. In actuality, your audience—even when they are in the same field or class as you—need just a few sentences of guidance where you explicitly state your purpose and scope. This is particularly important in job talks. Just because you sent part of your dissertation as a writing sample does not mean everyone in the room has read it or remembers it. A good trick for such situations is to begin by talking about how you got interested in the topic and describe how you transformed your curiosity into a research project.

Emphasize Main Ideas

Though I enjoy complex, nuanced, rich reports of research, in oral presentations especially, I need some sense from the speaker of what I should take from the talk. It really helps when a speaker uses numbers, in fact, to forecast what is to come (e.g., "I'm going to discuss four interesting findings from my study today.") Then, when introducing each one, it helps if the speaker uses the number again. This very simple approach keeps an audience with you. Your main ideas can still be complex and nuanced, but your presentation of them should be clear.

Define Your Terms

In my writing center, we use the term *multimodal* frequently. So frequently, actually, that I forget when I'm in other departments or at other schools that the term is not universally understood. Practice your presentation with someone unfamiliar with your research. Have him or her write down each term that needs more explanation.

Read Audience Cues

If you are doing a good job of talking from your notes instead of reading word for word, you'll be able to look at your audience. This provides you with instant feedback on what is interesting, confusing, or boring to them. Don't just use one person as a base, however; look around to see if you can discern the general mood.

Dwell on Data

Though oral presentations mean you must be selective about what you discuss in the given time period, I get the most from presentations that spend one-half to three-fourths of the dedicated time talking about findings and analysis.

Keep Your Body Calm, but Not Robotic

Audiences can be distracted by what you do with your body during the presentation and forget to pay attention to what you are saying. If you pace, twirl your hair, jingle your keys in your pocket, click your pen, sit on a table and swing your legs, or perform any other repetitive motion, your audience will find it difficult to concentrate.

Don't Self-Deprecate

When a speaker repeatedly tries to make fun of him or herself during a presentation, it often undercuts his or her authority. Humor can be effective, but I've rarely seen self-deprecation work well in a presentation.

Be Prepared for Tech Failure

You should certainly know what technology you will have available, but be ready to talk whether or not that technology works. If you have a particular data table or graphic that explains your entire study—or is the lynchpin for your entire presentation—then have it ready as a hardcopy handout in case the technology does not work during your presentation.

Practice Out Loud

Having your speaking materials prepared and try to shape your practice as closely to the real presentation as possible. Click through your slides as you talk. Pause when you will distribute handouts. This rehearsal will give you the closest estimate of how long your presentation will be. Moreover, once you have rehearsed your presentation a few times, you will be more familiar with the arrangement of ideas. If possible, practice your presentation with an audience.

Know What You Can Cut

When you practice, you might find that you are right on your time limit. That is good. But on the day of the presentation, there may be any number of time delays that cut into your presentation time—the door might be locked, the projector won't come on, the other speakers go over their time limits, and so on. So even when you know your material will fit in your time limit, you should also know what you can abbreviate or cut on the fly. You would not want to cut entire sections, say your methods section, because that might make your presentation incoherent. Instead, isolate a finding or an example that could be mentioned briefly instead of illustrated fully. Invite audience members to follow up on that point in the Q&A.

Be Ethical

It should go without saying that you should cite your secondary sources. But be clear in your speaking when the idea is yours and when you are quoting. Introduce quotations with the author's name and the title of the source. It's okay to say "quote" when you begin quoting a source and "end quote" when the quotation is complete for clarity.

If you have human subjects, do not violate your informed consent agreements with them during your presentation. If you have video footage of an interview that you told your participants you would only use to craft transcripts, it is not okay to show that footage during your talk. Review your IRB proposal, consent, and release forms before your presentation to remind yourself of the safeguards in place.

Though I've offered many suggestions in this chapter for reporting research, the piece of advice I would like readers to remember most is that fellow writing center scholars are interested and in fact excited to read your research. As writers, we sometimes can fall into a perfectionist trap and undervalue the work we have done. As a result, I think there is a lot of research that is conducted and never shared with other scholars. I'd encourage you to propose to conferences (writing center conferences and other related conferences too) and to submit manuscripts to journals. Doing so, your research has not only contributed to your own understandings of the work of writing centers but will also make a contribution to the field.

For Discussion, Reflection, and Action

1. Find a writing center research article (check the Works Cited if you want suggestions) and imagine that you are the author and have to condense the article into a fifteen-minute presentation. Imagine an audience for the presentation and develop a minute by minute outline of how long you will use your time. Then, imagine what visuals might be effective were you to deliver this presentation.

2. With the same research article or a different one, imagine how you might convey the information in different modes were you to develop a webtext. Are there particular modes that would work better for particular sections of your report? Or for particular findings? How do the different modes complicate your report (in a good way)?

Recommended Resources

Bishop, Wendy. *Ethnographic Writing Research: Writing it Down, Writing it Up, and Reading It.* Portsmouth, NH: Boynton/Cook, 1999. Print.
Gray, David. *Doing Research in the Real World.* 2nd ed. Thousand Oaks, CA: Sage, 2009. Print.
Stake, Robert. *Qualitative Research: Studying How Things Work.* New York: Guilford Press, 2010. Print.

Research Notebook #3: Beginning Analysis

Nikki Caswell, Rebecca Jackson, and
Jackie Grutsch McKinney

Like most qualitative researchers, we began our analysis almost immediately upon starting data collection and continued throughout the project but in perhaps a less conventional way. While qualitative researchers working in close proximity might meet with one another face-to-face on a set schedule, we used emails, texts, and phone calls to tell each other what we were hearing and speculating on what else we might hear and what it could mean to the project. We shared quotations from the interviews and told about particular snares our participants were in and particular successes they had.

The call for papers for the 2013 *Conference on College Composition and Communication* gave us an opportunity to examine the data from a particular theoretical perspective since the theme was "The Public Work of Composition." We used Erving Goffman's idea that we "perform self" in both "front stage" and "back stage" spaces and that the selves we perform in these spaces are often very different. We each did a more formal analysis, interpretation, and report of the first month's data for a presentation that fit well with the conference theme, and focused our first stage analysis.

After the conference, we continued to gather data, transcribe interviews, and conduct ongoing analysis. We got to a point at the end of our data collection where no clear path out seemed evident. We experienced what nearly every researcher does after completing data collection: paralysis. "There's so much!" we said to each other with both excitement and dread in our voices. We tried to figure out which data would be used in the project and couldn't agree. Eventually, Jackie made a trip to Texas to sit down with Rebecca to try to get unstuck. We had nine case studies and though we were shaping our report as a book-length project, we felt that nine cases might be too many for readers to follow if we dedicated a chapter to each participant. It would be like having nine main characters in a novel, we feared. We discussed how many book-length case studies and dissertations in writing (center) studies typically have four to six cases, yet even before we made the cut, we began, what Elizabeth Chiseri-Strater and Bonnie Sunstein call "grieving lost data" (154). Since we had spent a year in contact with each of our participants, it wasn't easy to let any of them go. As researchers, we had formed relationships with them and worried we wouldn't fulfill the tacit contract we had with each to make good use of the time and stories each had entrusted to us. Besides, we found each case utterly fascinating.

After a few hours at Rebecca's dining room table with Nikki on speaker phone, we started to see a way to keep all nine and still make analysis and reporting manageable. We realized the most useful way to begin analysis would be to sort our cases into types of positions they held: tenure-track faculty, full-time administrators, and part-time/ contingent positions. It was along these fault lines where we saw initial likenesses, and we felt that readers could follow along were the cases divided into chapters devoted to these three types. After figuring out a way to proceed we agreed to a schedule for completing transcriptions, sharing files, and drafting chapters.

We started coding transcripts separately and after a whole day together at a conference in the spring of 2014—including many hours at a long table in a hotel lobby—we were able to reduce our codes to a reasonable number and group those codes into themes or categories. We drafted a coding scheme and started applying it in a second pass of the data. Our analysis now has evolved away from the ideas of Goffman and toward a focus on the types of labor our participants described (which we're calling *everyday*, *emotional*, and *disciplinary*) and the needs that they describe for themselves as directors or for their centers. We also realized that grouping participants by job type wasn't entirely helpful anymore as it might force distinctions that were blurrier given our focus on labor and needs; that is, the participants' particular job classification was no longer a defining characteristic—all had each type of labor and different types of needs.

The act of returning to the data to read it in different ways was liberating because it provided confirmation that there is no one right way to make sense of the data. Furthermore, what initially felt like paralysis now feels more like possibility. We can dive in and out of the data, sorting it, and interpreting it in several ways for several different ends.

Glossary

Analysis: analysis refers to organizing and sorting data. Analysis is sometimes used synonymously with interpretation.

Backchannel cues: indications that listeners give verbally to conversation partners (e.g., "Yes" and "uh-huh").

Close vertical transcription: a style of transcription that shows graphically how and when speakers in conversations overlap. (See Appendix D.)

Coding: "the process of identifying units of analysis and classifying each unit according to the categories in a coding system—either a preexisting system or one developed for the data in question" (Grant-Davie 272). "The act of sorting and classifying data" (Blythe 204)

Confidence level: margin of error; used in reporting generalizable data. A common margin of error for surveys is three to five percent.

Confidence interval: The confidence level says my findings for my sample are likely for the whole population a certain percent of the time; a common confidence level for surveys is ninety-five percent.

Control group: the group in an experiment that does not get the treatment.

Convenience sampling: a means of selecting a sample from a larger population in which the researcher makes a selection based on available participants, not random sampling.

Corpus: a set of texts selected for review by the researcher.

Data: information the researcher collects to answer the research question. Grant-Davie says data is "any raw material or information gathered or observed in the course of a research project and considered relevant to the research" (271), and Haswell says data is "a once-occuring historical act that the researcher cannot change" (187).

Denaturalize: the process of trying to see something "normal" as strange or new.

Discourse analysis: the study of language in use—in written, gestural, or oral form.

Empirical inquiry: type of research which is the focus of this book; research where the researcher collects and interprets data.

Experimental research: research in which a test or experiment is conducted.

Fieldwork: a type of data collection during which the researcher observes and takes notes; may include participation, sketching, recording, activity logging, and interviewing.

Functional unit: a unit for coding that is based on what the chunk of text does rather than grammatical limits. Thus, a functional unit might be a talk turn as opposed to a sentence that is a syntactical unit.

Gaze: what one looks at. The researcher's gaze shapes the study, so researchers should pay attention to what they see and what they don't see, particularly at research sites where they are insiders.

Horizontal transcription: a style of transcription that show speakers taking turns talking. (See Appendix D.)

Inductive approach: gathering data before making interpretations

Informant check: the process of checking initial interpretations with participants in a study to see if what's noticed is in line with participant experience or perceptions.

Informed consent form: formally used to ask human subjects to take part in your study.

Interpretation: how the researcher makes sense of the data for others

Interrater reliability: having an outsider reader code a section of your data to see what percentage of the time you and the other reader agree upon codes.

IRB (Institutional Review Board): a group of people at universities and hospitals that must sanction research conducted at their institutions.

Latent codes: codes for which the researcher makes interpretation or inference.

Limitations: what your study or findings cannot say. All studies have limitations because of type of study, scope, time, budget, and access.

Literature review: the part of a research proposal or report that summarizes and synthesizes previous scholarship and research on the same topic and/or method.

Lore: received wisdom on a topic.

Manifest codes: codes that are evident in the data set (e.g., the repetition of a particular word).

Marker: a word, person, or event alluded to in one interview response that an interviewer returns to later after the question at hand is answered.

Method vs. methodology: many in writing studies use *method* to mean the procedure or technique for collecting data and *methodology* to mean the assumptions or theoretical frame of the researcher (Blythe 205).

Mixed-method: a study that uses both quantitative and qualitative methods.

Participant observation: an approach to fieldwork when the researcher participates in this scene.

Peer review: a process by which submissions are sent to a review board (usually anonymously or "blind") that decides whether or not the submission should be published.

Population: all of the people under consideration in a study (e.g., writing center clients); researchers often select a smaller sample to actually study within large populations.

Practitioner inquiry: scholarship in which an author uses his or her own experiences as evidence.

Probe: a response from the interviewer that invites that interviewee to continue discussing a particular point.

Qualitative research: research that interprets non-numeric data like words and images.

Quantitative research: research that interprets numeric data.

Random number generator: an online tool that essentially will draw numbers out of a hat—randomly select numbers from a given set.

Random sampling: selecting a sample from the larger population in which each member of the population must have an equal chance of being selected to participate.

Recruitment: the process for getting participants to take part in your study.

Release form: a form used to gain permission to use media (e.g., photos or videos) of participants within your research report.

Reliability: the notion that the study would yield the same findings each time it was executed by the same researcher or another.

Research problem: the gap between what is known and not known on a topic; a workable research problem must not have an easy answer and must not be unanswerable.

Research question: the exact question or questions the researcher wants to answer in a study. In experimental inquiry, a researcher uses a hypothesis instead.

Response rate: the percentage of recruited participants who actual participate in the study.

Sample: the smaller group from within the population under study that is selected for the study.

Sample size calculator: an online tool that allows a researcher to determine how large a sample must be to make generalizations of the entire population.

Secondary source: a source (e.g., article or book) found via library database, Web search or other means.

Significant: in quantitative research, a statistical term meaning that there is a mathematical difference discerned in the comparison.

Survey frame: list of all the members of a population used to find random samples.

Syntactic unit: a unit of analysis that is shaped by grammatical rules (e.g., phrases, T-units, sentences).

Talk turn: in conversational analysis, what is said in each exchange.

Theoretical inquiry: scholarship in which secondary sources are used for evidence.

Transcript: the word for word written representation of a recording.

Treatment: in experimental research, the treatment is the test or experiment. The treatment is not given to the control group.

Triangulation: making an interpretation from multiple data points.

Usability testing: engaging users with a particular site, tool, or document to see if users can complete specified tasks or to get opinions on the artifact under study.

Validity: a study is valid when it is planned and executed in such a way that it is able to answer its research question.

Notes

CHAPTER 1

1. Though Rhetoric and Composition has been the most common name for the field, writing studies as a term is increasing in popularity as the field moves from an almost exclusive focus on pedagogy to other studies of writing. This movement is described more in the last part of this chapter.

2. Since writing centers began in English departments, the case could also be made for the roots of practitioner inquiry in literary or expressive writing.

3. One can find writing center research prior to the 1980s; however, it wasn't until mechanisms like journals and conferences began that writing center studies started to coalesce as a field.

4. A related movement in Rhetoric and Composition—some would say a part of the post-process movement—that emerged in the late 1980s is ecocomposition. Influenced by Marilyn Cooper's "The Ecology of Writing," ecocomposition questions the role of spaces and places on writing—paying attention to natural, material, and social relationships between writers and places.

CHAPTER 2

5. As an alternative, many researchers are happy to email you a copy of their dissertation or thesis if you contact them.

6. Experimental research will have a hypothesis instead of a research question. Researchers using experimental design will predict what they will find in their hypothesis.

7. A nice overview of reliability and validity is available on the Writing@CSU website at: http://writing.colostate.edu/guides/guide. cfm?guideid=66.

CHAPTER 3

8. The debate on whether a tutor should be directive or non-directive in tutoring has been discussed frequently in writing center scholarship and research, as has the idea that ESL students might need different tutoring than students who have English as a first language.

9. Many students, for example, are encouraged in first-year writing courses to write in multiple modes as is the norm outside of academe; this is called multimodality or multimodal composition.

CHAPTER 4

10. The focus group instrument is available on their project website: http://www.writing.wisc.edu/pwtarp/.

CHAPTER 5

11. WCENTER is the listserv for writing center professionals and WPA-L is a listserv for writing program administrators (those individuals charged with overseeing first-year writing courses, majors and minors in writing, and/or writing across the curriculum programs). A listserv is an email distribution list that automatically sends any message to all the members on the list.

12. "Surveying" as a term also used to describe interviews and surveys of documents—two approaches discussed in other chapters. This chapter is about the method of distributing questions via questionnaires.

13. IRBs (as discussed in Chapter 2) will likely not sign off on a project that provides an incentive so attractive that it is deemed coercive.

14. It is possible to do a random sample of a large population without knowing the exact size of the population. Pollsters do this during election seasons when they poll likely voters in a particular state, for instance. There can be increased possibility of a sampling error in this situation because the researcher does not have a survey frame to select participants.

15. Population can be represented in research as a number with an italic upper-case N (e.g., N=3000). The sample is represented with an italic lower-case n (e.g., n=300).

16. The calculator will allow you to leave the population field blank if your population is very large or unknown. If I calculate an unknown population with a margin of error of five and a ninety-five percent confidence level, I need 384 participants.

17. Mary Sue MacNealey's discussion of sampling techniques is quite helpful (155–57).

18. A work-in-progress list of writing centers is compiled by St. Cloud State University and is available online.

19. It's possible to use the same sample size calculator mentioned in Note 16 to find a sample size even when the population size is unknown. In fact, Czaja and Blair note that "Population size does not affect sample size unless the population is small and the sample is more than 5% of the population" (132).

20. It is especially important for researchers to be sensitive to options available on demographic questions on race, gender, and language. It may be best on these questions (though perhaps a little more time consuming in analysis) to allow demographic questions to be blanks rather than multiple choices to avoid inadvertently making a participant feel invisible.

CHAPTER 6

21. Geiser and Slattery call the strategies frequently used in usability testing (think-aloud protocols, event logs, and video screen capture) *process-tracing methods* (197–98).

22. Bonnie Devet crafts an observation form that could be a sort of model for a tutoring activity log in "A Method for Observing and Evaluating Writing Lab Tutorials."

23. See James Paul Gee's *The Anti-Education Era* for an interesting discussion of this human tendency.

CHAPTER 7

24. Only one published account of writing center action research could be located—Cathy Hutchins's article mentioned later in this chapter. However, there are two writing center sources that encourage the use of action research (Godbee and Ozias; Bell) and a recent *Writing Center Journal* article, "Empowering L2 Tutoring: A Case Study of a Second Language Writer's Vocabulary Learning" that asserts a tutor-research methodology.

CHAPTER 8

25. Stuart Blythe reminds us, however, that so called "raw" data is data that has been purposefully collected by us for the purposes of our study, so our selection of some data over others ought to complicate our understanding of raw or untouched data.

26. As with most things in the research process, there are many possibilities here. A chunk could be a paragraph, a sentence, or a talk turn, depending on what seems useful and feasible for your study. Most approaches to coding suggest every chunk be given at least one code, so do not make your chunks too small so as to make this task impossible.

27. Auerbach and Silverstein do concede that you might have "orphans"—bits of data that do not repeat yet that you don't want to dismiss (58–59). They say orphans can be used in reporting your findings if you are clear that it corresponds to only one person or instance.

Works Cited

Auerbach, Carl, and Louise Silverstein. *Qualitative Data: An Introduction to Coding and Analysis*. New York: New York UP, 2003. Print.

Babcock, Rebecca, Kellye Manning, Travis Rogers, and Courtney Goff. *A Synthesis of Qualitative Studies of Writing Center Tutoring, 1983–2006*. Peter Lang, 2012. Print.

Balester, Valerie, and James McDonald. "A View of Status and Working Conditions: Relations Between Writing Program and Writing Center Directors." *WPA* 24.3 (2001): 59–82. PDF.

Bazerman, Charles, and David Russell. *Writing Selves/Writing Societies: Research from Activity Perspectives*. Fort Collins, CO: WAC Clearinghouse, 2003. Online.

Bell, Diana Calhous, and Madeleine Youmans. "Politeness and Praise: Rhetorical Issues in ESL (L2) Writing Center Conferences." *Writing Center Journal* 26.2 (2006): 31–47. PDF.

Bell, Jim. "What Are We Talking About?: A Content Analysis of the Writing Lab Newsletter, April 1985-October 1988." *Writing Lab Newsletter* 13.7 (1989): 1–4. PDF.

Bishop, Wendy. *Ethnographic Writing Research: Writing it Down, Writing it Up, and Reading It*. Portsmouth, NH: Boynton/Cook, 1999. Print.

—. "Bringing Writers to the Center: Some Survey Results, Surmises, and Suggestions." *Writing Center Journal* 10.2 (1990): 31–45. PDF.

Black, Laurel Johnson. *Between Talk and Teaching*. Logan, UT: Utah State UP, 1997. Print.

Blakeslee, Ann, and Cathy Fleischer. *Becoming a Writing Researcher*. Mahwah, NJ: Erlbaum, 2007. Print.

Blau, Susan, John Hall, Jeff Davis, and Lauren Gravitz. "Tutoring ESL Students: A Different Kind of Session" *Writing Lab Newsletter* 25.10 (2001): 1–4. PDF.

Blau, Susan, John Hall, and Tracy Strauss. "Exploring the Tutor/Client Conversation: A Linguistic Analysis." *Writing Center Journal* 19.1 (1998): 19–48. PDF.

Bloom, Leslie Rebecca. "From Self to Society: Reflections on the Power of Narrative Inquiry." *Qualitative Research in Practice: Examples for Discussion and Analysis.* Ed. Sharon Merriam. San Francisco, CA: Jossey-Bass, 2002. Print.

Blythe, Stuart. "Coding Digital Texts and Multimedia." *Digital Writing Research.* Ed. Heidi McKee and Danielle DeVoss. New York: Hampton Press, 2007. Print.

Blythe, Stuart, Jeffrey Grabill, and Kirk Riley. "Action Research and Wicked Environmental Problems." *Journal of Business and Technical Communication.* 22.3 (2008): 272-98. PDF.

Boquet, Elizabeth, and Neal Lerner. "After 'The Idea of a Writing Center.'" *College English* 71.2 (2008): 170–89. PDF.

Boquet, Elizabeth. *Noise from the Writing Center.* Logan, UT: Utah State UP, 2002. Print.

Brazeau, Alicia. "Groupies and Singletons: Student Preferences in Classroom-Based Writing Consulting." *Young Scholars in Writing* 2 (2004): 46–55. Online.

Brown, Robert. "Representing Audiences in Writing Center Consultation: A Discourse Analysis." *Writing Center Journal* 30.2 (2010): 72–99. PDF.

Bruffee, Kenneth. "Collaborative Learning and the 'Conversation of Mankind.'" *Cross-Talk in Comp Theory.* 2nd ed. Ed. Victor Villanueva. Urbana, IL: NCTE, 2003. 415-36. Print.

Buck, Amber. "The Invisible Interface: MS Word in the Writing Center." *Computers and Composition* 25.4 (2008): 396–414. PDF.

Calhoun, Emily. *How to Use Action Research in the Self Renewing School.* Alexandria, VA: Association for Supervision and Curriculum Development, 1994. Print.

Canagarajah, Suresh. "Autoethnography in the Study of Multilingual Writers." *Writing Studies Research in Practice.* Ed. Lee Nickoson and Mary P. Sheridan. Carbondale, IL: Southern Illinois UP, 2012. 113–124. Print.

Carino, Peter, and Doug Enders. "Does Frequency of Visits to the
    Writing Center Increase Student Satisfaction? A Statistical Correla-
    tion Study—or Story." *Writing Center Journal* 21.3 (2001): 83–103.
    PDF.

Carino, Peter. "Early Writing Centers: Towards a History." *Writing
    Center Journal* 15.2 (1995): 103-16. PDF.

Carson, Terrance, and Dennis Sumara, eds. *Action Research as a Living
    Practice.* New York: Peter Lang, 1997. Print.

Charmaz, Kathy. *Constructing Grounded Theory.* Thousand Oaks,
    CA: Sage, 2006. Print.

Chiseri-Strater, Elizabeth, and Bonnie Sunstein. *What Works? A Prac-
    tical Guide for Teacher Research.* Portsmouth, NH: Heinemann,
    2006. Print.

Clark, Irene Lurkis. "Leading the Horse: The Writing Center and Re-
    quired Visits." *Writing Center Journal* 5.2 (1985): 31–35. PDF.

Conard-Salvo, Tammy, and John M. Spartz "Listening to Revise:
    What a Study about Text-to-Speech Software Taught Us about
    Students' Expectations for Technology Use in the Writing Center."
    Writing Center Journal 32.1 (2012): 40–59.

Condon, Frankie. *I Hope I Join the Band: Narrative, Affiliation, and
    Antiracist Rhetoric.* Logan, UT: Utah State UP, 2012. Print.

Cooper, Marilyn. "The Ecology of Writing." *College English* 48.4
    (1986): 364–75. PDF.

Corbett, Stephen. "Using Case Study Multi- Methods to Investigate
    Close(r) Collaboration: Course-based Tutoring and the Directive/
    Nondirective Instructional Continuum." *Writing Center Journal*
    31.1 (2011): 55–81. PDF.

Cresswell, John. *Research Design.* 4th ed. Thousand Oaks, CA: Sage,
    2013. Print.

Culhane, Alys. "The Seldom Heard Voices in Mary Lyon Basement:
    An Interview with Three College Writing Center Consultants."
    WAC Journal 11 (2000): 87–95. PDF.

Czaja, Ronald, and Johnny Blair. *Designing Surveys.* 2nd ed. Thousand
    Oaks, CA: Sage, 2004. Print.

Denny, Harry. *Facing the Center.* Logan, UT: Utah State UP, 2010.
    Print

Dickens, Linda, and Karen Watkins. "Action Research: Rethinking
    Lewin." *Management Learning* 30.2 (1999): 127-40. PDF.

Dipardo, Anne. "'Whispers of Coming and Going': Lessons from Fannie." *Writing Center Journal* 12.2 (1992): 125-45. PDF.

Dobrin, Sid, J. A. Rice, and Michael Vastola. *Beyond Postprocess*. Logan, UT: Utah State UP, 2011. Print.

Driscoll, Dana Lynn, and Sherry Wynn Perdue. "Theory, Lore, and More: An Analysis of RAD Research in the *Writing Center Journal*, 1980–2009." *Writing Center Journal* 32.1 (2012): 11–39.

Elbow, Peter. *Writing Without Teachers*. 2nd ed. New York, NY: Oxford UP, 1998. Print.

Emerson, Robert, Rachel Fretz, and Linda Shaw. *Writing Ethnographic Fieldnotes*. Chicago, IL: U of Chicago P, 1995. Print.

Faber, Brenton. *Community Action and Organizational Change: Image, Narrative, Identity*. Carbondale, IL: Southern Illinois UP, 2002. Print.

Flower, Linda, and John Hayes. "A Cognitive Process Theory of Writing." *Cross-Talk in Comp Theory*. 2nd ed. Ed. Victor Villanueva. Urbana, IL: NCTE, 2003. 273-98. Print.

Gee, James Paul. *How to Do Discourse Analysis*. New York, NY: Routledge, 2010. Print.

Geisler, Cheryl, and Shaun Slattery. "Capturing the Activity of Digital Writing: Using, Analyzing, and Supplementing Video Screen Capture." *Digital Writing Research*. Ed. Heidi McKee and Danielle DeVoss. Hampton Press, 2007. Print.

Geller, Anne Ellen, Michelle Eodice, Frankie Condon, Meg Carroll and Beth Boquet. *The Everyday Writing Center*. Logan, UT: Utah State UP, 2006. Print.

Gillespie, Paula, Brad Hughes, and Harvey Kail. "What They Take with Them: Findings from the Peer Writing Tutor Alumni Research Project." *Writing Center Journal* 30.2 (2010): 12–46. PDF.

-----. "Focus Groups." *Peer Tutoring Alumni Research Project*. Web. 17 Aug. 2015.

Gilewicz, Magdalena, and Terese Thonus. "Close Vertical Transcription in Writing Center Training and Research." *Writing Center Journal* 24.1 (2003): 25–49. PDF.

Glaser, Bernie, and Anselm Strauss. *The Discovery of Grounded Theory*. Mill Valley, CA: Sociology Press, 1967. Print.

Godbee, Beth, and Moira Ozias. "Organizing for Antiracism in Writing Centers: Principles for Enacting Social Change." *Writing Cen-

ters and the New Racism. Ed. Laura Greenfield and Karen Rowan. Logan, UT: Utah UP, 2011. Print.

Grabill, Jeffrey. *Community Literacy Programs and the Politics of Change.* Albany, NY: SUNY P, 2001. Print.

Grady, Michael. *Qualitative and Action Research.* Bloomington, IN: Phi Delta Kappa International, 1998. Print.

Grant-Davie, Kevin. "Coding Data: Issues of Validity, Reliability, and Interpretation." *Methods and Methodology in Composition Research.* Ed. Gesa Kirsch and Patricia A. Sullivan. Carbondale, IL: Southern Illinois UP, 1992. 270-86. Print.

Gray, David. *Doing Research in the Real World.* 2nd ed. Thousand Oaks, CA: Sage, 2009. Print.

Greenfield, Laura and Karen Rowan. *Writing Centers and the New Racism.* Logan, UT: Utah State UP, 2011. Print.

Griffin, Gabrielle, ed. *Research Methods for English Studies.* Edinburgh: Edinburgh UP, 2006. Print.

Grimm, Nancy. *Good Intentions: Writing Center Work for Postmodern Times.* New York, NY: Heinemann, 1999. Print.

Griswold, W. Gary. "Postsecondary Reading: What Writing Center Tutors Need to Know." *Journal of College Reading and Learning* 37.1 (2006): 61–72. PDF.

Grutsch McKinney, Jackie. "Geek in the Center: Twitter." *Writing Lab Newsletter* 35.3 (Nov/Dec 2010): 6–9. PDF.

Hardy, Melissa, and Alan Bryman. *Handbook of Data Analysis.* Thousand Oaks, CA: Sage, 2004. Print.

Harris, Joseph. *A Teaching Subject.* New Edition. Logan, UT: Utah State UP, 2012. Print.

Hart-Davidson, Bill. "Studying the Mediated Action of Composing with Time-Use Diaries." *Digital Writing Research.* Ed. Heidi McKee and Danielle DeVoss. Hampton Press, 2007. 153-70. Print.

Haswell, Richard. "NCTE/CCCC's Recent War on Scholarship." *Written Communication* 22 (2005): 198–223. PDF.

—. "Quantitative Methods in Composition Studies: An Introduction to Their Functionality." *Writing Studies Research in Practice.* Ed. Lee Nickoson and Mary P. Sheridan. Edwardsville, IL: Southern Illinois UP, 2012. Print.

Heath, Shirley Brice. *Ways with Words: Language, Life and Work in Communities and Classrooms.* New York, NY: Cambridge UP, 1983. Print.

Hemmeter, Tom, and Carolyn Mee. "The Writing Center as Ethnographic Space" *Writing Lab Newsletter* (1993): 4–5. PDF.

Hensley Owens, Kim and Van Ittersum, Derek. ('Writing With(out) Pain: Computing Injuries and the Role of the Body in Writing Activity." *Computers and Composition,* 30.2 (2013): 87–100.

Hesse-Biber, Sharlene Nagy, and Patricia Leavy. *The Practice of Qualitative Research.* 2nd ed. Thousand Oaks, CA: Sage, 2011.

Holstein, James, and Jaber F. Gubrium. *The Active Interview.* Qualitative Research Methods Series 37. Thousand Oaks, CA: Sage, 1995.

Huckin, Thomas. "Context Sensitive Text Analysis." *Methods and Methodology in Composition Research.* Ed. Gesa Kirsch, and Patricia A. Sullivan. Carbondale, IL: Southern Illinois UP, 1992. 84–104. Print.

Hunzer, Kathleen. "Misperceptions of gender in the writing center: Stereotyping and the facilitative tutor." *Writing Lab Newsletter* 22.2 (1997): 6–10. PDF.

Hutchings, Cathy. "Reaching Students: Lessons from a Writing Centre." *Higher Education Research and Development* 25.3 (2006): 247-61. PDF.

Ianetta, Melissa, Michael McCampley, and Catherine Quick. "Taking Stock: Surveying the Relationship of the Writing Center and TA Training." *WPA* 31.1–2 (2007): 104-23. PDF.

Jackson, Rebecca, Carrie Leverenz, and Joe Law. "(Re) shaping the Profession: Graduate Courses in Writing Center Theory, Practice, and Administration." *The Center Will Hold.* Ed. Michael Pemberton and Joyce Kinkead. Logan, UT: Utah State UP, 2003. 130-50. Print.

Jackson, Rebecca, and Jackie Grutsch McKinney. "Beyond Tutoring: Mapping the Invisible Landscape of Writing Center Work." *Praxis: A Writing Center Journal.* 9.1 Web. 2011. 25 July 2015.

Johanek, Cindy. *Composing Research.* Logan, UT: Utah State UP, 2000. Print.

Johnson, Andrew. *A Short Guide to Action Research.* 3rd ed. New York: Longman, 2007. Print.

Johnstone, Barbara. *Discourse Analysis.* 2nd ed. Malden, MA: Blackwell, 2002. Print.

Learner, Neal. "Insider as Outsider: Participant Observation as Writing Center Research." *Writing Center Research: Extending the Con-*

versation. Ed. Paula Gillespie, Alice Gillam, Lady Falls Brown, and Byron Stay. Mahwah, NJ: Erlbaum, 2002. Print.

LeCompte, Margaret, and Jean Schensul. *Analyzing and Interpreting Ethnographic Data.* Lanham, MD: Altamira Press, 1999. Print.

Liggett, Sarah, Kerri Jordan, and Steve Price. "Makers of Knowledge in Writing Centers: Practitioners, Scholars, and Researchers at Work." *The Changing of Knowledge in Composition.* Ed. Lance Massey and Richard Gebhardt. Logan, UT: Utah State UP, 2011. 102-20. Print.

Liggett, Sarah, Kerri Jordan, and Steve Price. "Mapping Knowledge-Making in Writing Center Research: A Taxonomy of Methodologies." *Writing Center Journal* 31.2 (2011): 50–88. PDF.

McCarthy, Meesh, and Erin O'Brien. "Check One: Tutor Hat, Teacher Hat, Facilitator Hat, Some/All/None of the Above." *Human Architecture: Journal of the Sociology of Self-Knowledge* 6.1 (2008): 27–44. PDF.

McLellen, Eleanor, Kathleen McQueen, and Judith Neidig. "Beyond the Qualitative Interview: Data Preparation and Transcription." *Field Methods* 15.1 (2003): 63–84. PDF.

Mackiewicz, Jo, and Isabelle Thompson. "Motivational Scaffolding, Politeness, and Writing Center Tutoring." *Writing Center Journal* 33.1 (2013): 38–73. PDF.

MacNealey, Mary Sue. *Strategies for Empirical Research in Writing.* Boston, MA: Longman, 1998. Print.

Melnick, Jane. "The Politics of Writing Conferences: Describing Authority Through Speech Act Theory." *Writing Center Journal* 4.2 (1984): 9–22. PDF.

Meyers, Sharon. "Reassessing The 'Proofreading Trap': ESL Tutoring and Writing Instruction." *Writing Center Journal* 24.1 (2003): 51–70. PDF.

Morrison, Julie Bauer, and Jean-Paul Nadeau. "How Was Your Session at the Writing Center? Pre- and Post-Grade Student Evaluations." *Writing Center Journal* 23.2 (2003): 25–42. PDF.

Mortensen, Peter. "Analyzing Talk about Writing." *Methods and Methodology in Composition Research.* Ed. Gesa Kirsch, Gesa and Patricia A. Sullivan. Carbondale, IL: Southern Illinois UP, 1992. Print.

Mould, David. "Interviewing." *Catching Stories: A Practical Guide to Oral History.* Ed. Donna DeBlasio, Charles Ganzert, David

Mould, Stephen Paschen, and Howard Sacks. Athens, OH: Ohio UP, 2009. Print. 82–103.

Murphy, Susan Wolff. "'Just Chuck It: I Mean, Don't Get Fixed On It': Self-Presentation in Writing Center Discourse." *Writing Center Journal* 26.1 (2006): 62–82. PDF.

Murray, Donald. "Teaching Writing as a Process Not Product." *Cross-Talk in Comp Theory.* 2nd ed. Ed. Victor Villanueva. Urbana, IL: NCTE, 2003. 3–6. Print.

Neulieb, Janice Witherspoon, and Maurice A. Scharton. "Writing Others, Writing Ourselves: Ethnography and the Writing Center." *Intersections: Theory-Practice in the Writing Center.* Ed. Joan Mullin and Ray Wallace. Urbana, IL: NCTE, 1994.

Neff, Joyce. "Capturing Complexity: Using Grounded Theory to Study Writing Centers." *Writing Center Research: Extending the Conversation.* Ed. Paula Gillespie, Alice Gillam, Lady Falls Brown, and Byron Stay. ; Mahwah, NJ: Erlbaum, 2002. 133-48. Print.

North, Stephen. "Writing Center Research: Testing Our Assumptions." *Writing Centers: Theory and Administration.* Ed. Gary Olson. Urbana, IL: NCTE, 1984. 24–35. Print.

——. "The Idea of a Writing Center." *College English* 42.5 (1984): 433-46. PDF.

O'Leary, Claire Elizabeth. "It's Not What You Say, But How You Say It (And to Whom): Accommodating Gender in the Writing Conference." *Young Scholars in Writing 6* (2008): NP. Online.

Perl, Sondra. "The Composing Processes of Unskilled College Writers." *Cross-Talk in Comp Theory.* 2nd ed. Ed. Victor Villanueva. Urbana, IL: NCTE, 2003. 17–42. Print.

Petric, Bojana. "Student's Attitudes Toward Writing and the Development of Academic Writing Skills." *Writing Center Journal* 22.2 (2002): 9–27. PDF.

Phillips, Talinn. "Tutor Training and Services for Multilingual Graduate Writers: A Reconsideration." *Praxis: A Writing Center Journal* 10.2. Web. 2013. 25 July 2015.

Ramsey, Birgitta. "Re-seeing the Writing Center's Position of Service." *Writing Lab Newsletter* 29.6 (2005): 1–5. PDF.

Raymond, Laurel, and Zarah Quinn. "What a Writer Wants: Assessing Fulfillment of Student Goals in Writing Center Tutoring Sessions." *Writing Center Journal* 32.1 (2012): 64–77.

Reigstad, Tom. "The Writing Conference: An Ethnographic Model for Discovering Patterns of Teacher-Student Interaction" *Writing Center Journal* 2.1 (1982) 9–21. PDF.

Restaino, Jessica. *First Semester: Graduate Students, Teaching Writing, and the Challenge of Middle Ground.* Urbana, IL: NCTE, 2012. Print.

Rosner, Mary, and Regan Wann. "Talking Heads and Other Body Parts." *Writing Lab Newsletter* 34.6 (2010): 7–11. PDF.

Rowan, Karen S. "Beyond the Anecdotal: Questioning Assumptions about Graduate Student Administrators." *The Writing Lab Newsletter* 31.6 (2007): 1–6. PDF.

—. "All the Best Intentions: Graduate Student Administrative Professional Development in Practice." *Writing Center Journal* 29.1 (2009): 11–48. PDF.

Rubin, Herbert, and Irene Rubin. *Qualitative Interviewing: The Art of Hearing Data.* 2nd Ed. Thousand Oaks, CA: Sage, 2005.

Schendel, Ellen. "We Don't Proofread, So What Do We Do? A Report on Survey Results" *Writing Lab Newsletter* 37.3–4 (2012): 1–6. PDF.

Schiely, Lauren. "Sharing Our Stories: Using Narrative Inquiry to Examine Our Writing Centers." MA Thesis. Texas State University-San Marcos, 2013. PDF.

Seidman, Irvin. *Interviewing as Qualitative Research.* 2nd ed. New York, NY: Teachers College Press, 1998. Print.

Severino, Carol. "Rhetorically Analyzing Collaborations." *Writing Center Journal* 13.1 (1992): 53–64. PDF.

Shea, Kelly. "Through the Eyes of the OWL: Assessing Faculty vs. Peer Tutoring in an Online Setting." *Writing Lab Newsletter* 35.7 (2011): 6–9. PDF.

Sheridan, Dave, and James Inman, eds. *Multiliteracy Centers.* New York, NY: Hampton Press, 2010. Print.

Sheridan, Mary. "Making Ethnography Our Own: Why and How Writing Studies Must Redefine Core Research Practices." *Writing Studies Research in Practice.* Ed. Lee Nickoson and Mary P. Sheridan. Carbondale, IL: Southern Illinois UP, 2012. 73–85. Print.

Smitherman, Carey. "Conducting an Oral History of Your Own Writing Center." *Writing Lab Newsletter* 27.10 (2003): 1–4. PDF.

Snively, Helen, Traci Freeman, and Cheryl Prentice. "Writing Centers for Graduate Students." *The Writing Center Director's Resource*

Book. Ed. Christina Murphy and Bryon Stay. Mahwah, NJ: Erlbaum, 2006.

Sommers, Nancy. "Revision Strategies of Student Writers and Experienced Adult Writers." *Cross-Talk in Comp Theory*. 2nd ed. Ed. Victor Villanueva. Urbana, IL: NCTE, 2003. 43–53. Print.

Standridge, Emily. "Characterizing Writing Tutorials." Dissertation. Ball State University, 2012.

Stake, Robert. *Qualitative Research: Studying How Things Work*. New York, NY: Guilford Press, 2010. Print.

Stringer, Ernest. *Action Research*. 3rd ed. Los Angeles, CA: Sage, 2007. Print.

Isabelle Thompson, Alyson Whyte, David Shannon, Amanda Muse, Kristen Miller, Milla Chappell, and Abby Whigham. "Examining Our Lore: A Survey of Students' and Tutors' Satisfaction with Writing Center Conferences." *Writing Center Journal* 29.1 (2009): 78–105.

Thonus, Therese. "Triangulation in the Writing Center: Tutor, Tutee, and the Instructor Perceptions of the Tutor's Role." *Writing Center Journal* 22.1 (2001): 59–82. PDF.

Trimbur, John. "Taking the Social Turn: Teaching Writing Post-Process." *College Composition and Communication* 45.1 (1994):108–18. PDF.

Van Ittersum, Derek. "Distributing Memory: Rhetorical Work in Digital Environments." *Technical Communication Quarterly* 18.3 (2009): 259-80.

Wilson, Nancy Effinger. "Bias in the Writing Center." *Writing Centers and the New Racism*. Ed. Laura Greenfield and Karen Rowan. Logan, UT: Utah State UP, 2011. Print. 177–91.

Woolbright, Meg. "The Politics of Tutoring: Feminism within the Patriarchy." *Writing Center Journal* 13.1 (1993): 16–31. PDF.

Young, Beth Rapp, and Barbara Fritzsche. "Writing Center Users Procrastinate Less: The Relationship Between Individual Differences in Procrastination, Peer Feedback, and Student Writing Process." *Writing Center Journal* 23.1 (2002): 45–58. PDF.

Appendix A: Sample Informed Consent Form

This is the informed consent form used for the study reflected on in the Research Notebook. Since we collected data at a distance, we had to email the forms to our participants and ask them to return them digitally or by mail before we started our interviews. The headings and much of the wording is boilerplate as directed by the IRBs at our home institutions. Let this serve as a sample, but consult your own IRB for requirements.

Study Title: Case Studies of New Writing Center Directors

Researchers

Nikki Caswell [East Carolina University]
Jackie Grutsch McKinney [Ball State University]
Rebecca Jackson [Texas State University-San Marcos]

Study Purpose and Rationale

This study hopes to explore how new writing center directors navigate their jobs. No existing, longitudinal study of this type has been completed. Findings will be important for the training of next generation writing center directors.

Inclusion/Exclusion Criteria

- You must be 18 years or older to participate.
- You must be in the first or second year of administrating a writing center.

- You must be willing to participate in interviews once monthly for the academic year 2012–2013.

Participation Procedures and Duration

- Participants will be interviewed once each month by email, phone, Skype, or chat from September 2012-May 2013.
- Researchers will record and transcribe interviews; transcripts will be shared with participants. Researchers will also take notes during the interview (when applicable).
- Participants will be encouraged to use a shared digital file to note important events/concerns to discuss at future interviews.

Audio Recording

For purposes of accuracy, the interviews will be audio recorded (when applicable). The recordings will be transcribed and shared among the research team. The transcript will be shared with the participants for fact checking. Once transcribed, a pseudonym will be ascribed to the transcript so that no identifiable information will be attached to the comments. The recordings will stored as password protected digital files until transcription is complete; files will then be deleted.

Data Confidentiality and Storage of Data

Data will be maintained confidentially on password protected digital files accessible only by the research team. All participants will be assigned a pseudonym; the pseudonym will be used in the data. Data will be maintained for 5 years and then deleted.

Risks or Discomforts

There are no anticipated risks for participating in this study.

Benefits

Participants will be given space and time to reflect on their experiences in their new jobs.

Voluntary Participation

Your participation in this study is completely voluntary and you are free to withdraw your permission at anytime for any reason without penalty or prejudice from the investigator. Please feel free to ask any questions of the investigator before signing this form and at any time during the study.

IRB Contact Information

For questions about your rights as a research subject, please contact Director, Office of Research Integrity, Ball State University, Muncie, IN 47306, (765) 285–5070, irb@bsu.edu.

Study Title: Case Studies of New Writing Center Directors

Researchers:
Nikki Caswell [East Carolina University]
Jackie Grutsch McKinney [Ball State University]
Rebecca Jackson [Texas State University-San Marcos]

****

Consent

I, _____, agree to participate in this research project entitled, "Case Studies of New Writing Center Directors." I have had the study explained to me and my questions have been answered to my satisfaction. I have read the description of this project and give my consent to participate. I understand that I will receive a copy of this informed consent form to keep for future reference.

I understand my participation in this study is completely voluntary and I am free to withdraw your permission at anytime for any reason without penalty or prejudice from the research team.

To the best of my knowledge, I meet the inclusion/exclusion criteria for participation (described on the previous page) in this study.

By signing, I give my permission for the research team to record interviews.

_____

Participant's Signature   Date
[Researcher Contact Information]

Appendix B: Sample Release Form

For any projects where the researcher intends to use the media used for data collection in the presentation of the research (photographs, video or audio recordings, screen captures), the researcher should obtain a release form. The sample release form below is adapted from one created by the Office of Research and Sponsored Projects at San Francisco State University. Other similar release forms can be found online. You will need to adapt the form to the particular type of media you are using.

Research Project:
Researcher(s):

PHOTO RELEASE FORM

As part of this project, I will be taking photographs of you (or your child) during your participation in the research. Please indicate what uses of these photographs you are willing to permit, by putting your initials next to the uses you agree to, and signing the form at the end. I will only use the photographs in ways that you agree to. In any use of the recordings, you (or your child) will not be identified by name, but by a pseudonym.

1. __The photographs can be studied by the research team for use in the research project.

2. __The photographs can be used in print or digital academic publications.

3. __The photographs can be shown at academic conferences or meetings.

4. __The photographs can be shown in classrooms to students.

5. __The photographs can be shown in public presentations to non-scientific groups.

6. __The photographs can be shown for training purposes to writing center staff.

7. __The photographs can be posted to a website or social media site.

I have read the above descriptions and give my consent for the use of the photographs as indicated by my initials above.

Printed Name_____

_____

(Signature)   (Date)

Appendix C: Driscoll and Perdue's RAD Rubric

In their article, "Theory, Lore, and More: An Analysis of RAD Research in the Writing Center Journal," Dana Driscoll and Sherry Wynn Perdue studied existing writing center research to determine how much RAD (replicable, aggregable, and data supported research) has been published in Writing Center Journal.* *During their study, they created and used this rubric to determine which articles were to higher and lower degree RAD studies. The rubric is also helpful for researchers to use when crafting and reporting their research; researchers can use it as a way to gauge their own progress.*

AREA 1: BACKGROUND AND SIGNIFICANCE

High (2): Clearly situates the study within the context of the field and previous literature, identifies the gap addressed by the work, and provides timely references to recent scholarship.

Medium (1): Provides some study contextualization and uses references, but discussion may not be thorough, timely, and detailed and may lack important information.

Low (0): Little or no relevant research related to the study is discussed, little to no contextualization and/or little to no discussion of a gap addressed.

AREA 2: STUDY DESIGN AND DATA COLLECTION

High (2): Methods are detailed enough that study could be reliably replicated in a new context. Methods section describes data collection, gives justification for methodological choices and how those choices relate to the study objectives, and identifies and describes research questions or hypotheses. Researchers make methodological choices that do not introduce bias into data collection, analysis, and description of results and/or make justifiable attempts to address and control for bias.

Medium (1): Some methodological description is present, but discussion lacks details in several of the categories (objectives, study design). Researchers may not provide justification of methodological choices but still present enough information about methods that replication could occur.

Low (0): No method section present, or methods described are so vague that study could not be reliability replicated.

AREA 3: SELECTION OF PARTICIPANTS AND/OR TEXTS

High (2): Selection of participants or texts is clear and justified. For surveys, quasi-experiments, or experiments, selection includes a discussion of random selection or sampling technique. For case studies, interviews, observations, or other qualitative work, description of the participant selection and representativeness of participants is present (i.e., participants are randomly chosen or chosen to represent a specific background, such as an ESL student). For textual analysis, a description of the selection process and sampling is clear and detailed.

Medium (1): Some discussion of the selection of participants or texts is present although information is unclear or incomplete. Justification of selection choices may not be present.

Low (0): Insufficient or no description and justification of participant or text selection.

AREA 4: METHOD OF ANALYSIS

High (2): Method of data analysis is clear, is fitting of the study design, and is meaningful. Categories of analysis and operational definitions are presented and described. Researchers provide evidence that analysis was done in a systematic manner.

Medium (1): Method of analysis is fairly clear and systematic, but missing detail in one or two key areas. It may not contain justifications.

Low (0): Insufficient or no description of the method of analysis. Researchers give no indication that analysis was done in a systematic manner.

Area 5: Presentation of Results

High (2): Results are presented in a clear and accessible manner. Results are supplemented by appropriate graphics, excerpts from texts or interviews, or other evidence. Results are presented in a manner that clearly separates them from discussion/opinions of the researcher.

Medium (1): Results are presented accurately, but there may be some confusion or areas where the results are unclear or are not supported with appropriate evidence. The distinction between results and discussion may be unclear in parts. Biased language in results may be present (for example, value judgments or interpretations of what participants were thinking rather than actual observed behavior).

Low (0): Insufficient description of results and/or results presented in a confusing, obtuse, or biased manner. No clear distinction between results and discussion is present.

Area 6: Discussion and Implications

High (2): Authors provide a clear description of how the results of the research contributes to the field's understanding of the issue and how the current study informs, complicates, or extends previous work (if any). Authors provide clear implications of the study and discuss broader applications of the results.

Medium (1): Authors provide some discussion of the results of the work within the context of the field, implications, and applications of the results, although parts of this discussion may be missing or lack sufficient detail.

Low (0): Insufficient and/or no discussion of implications or broader applications.

AREA 7: LIMITATIONS AND FUTURE WORK

High (2): Researchers give clear suggestions for future work that they or others may pursue relating to the study results and provide clear acknowledgement of study limitations.

Medium (1): Researchers give some suggestions for future work and some acknowledgement of study limitations. Overstatements about the value of the work may also be present.

Low (0): Insufficient discussion of study limitations or future work. (21–23)

*Adapted from Driscoll, Dana Lynn, and Sherry Wynn Perdue. "Theory, Lore, and More: An Analysis of RAD Research in the *Writing Center Journal,* 1980–2009." *Writing Center Journal* 32.1 (2012): 11–39. Used with permission.

Appendix D: Transcriptions

The more you read writing center research, the more you'll notice there are different conventions for transcriptions, meaning there are different ways that writers try to represent oral speech in writing. There is not one right way to do transcription; your transcription is not a pure reproduction of a conversation or interview. It is a representation. As researcher, you make choices with your transcription style for what you want to represent and what you don't.

If you are simply interested in showing *what* a respondent said, you might use a style that resembles dialogue in a play. This is sometimes called **horizontal transcription** and is seen in this excerpt from *Research Methods for English Studies:*

> **But playwrights like Caryl Churchill started off something that was non-linear and different, that moved away from one central character.**
>
> Yes, in that respect Caryl Churchill is Picasso.
>
> **Why do you think you are accused of using improbable scenarios and dialogue?**
>
> It's difficult to answer this without knowing which scenes and what dialogue it refers to.
>
> The easy answer would be . . . (Griffin 189):

Note in this example that the question is in bold and the answer is in regular type; other sources might format it differently. Both the question and answer are written in complete sentences with no non-verbal information provided, no filler words, and no pauses indicated. Horizontal transcriptions may or may not include these.

If you are interested in the interaction of two (or more) people—in representing where two speakers overlapped or interrupted one another, you might use **close vertical transcription**. This type of transcription is described in Mary Rosner and Regan Wann's "Talking Heads and Other Body Parts" and Magdalena Gilewicz and Terese Thonus's "Close Vertical Transcription in Writing Center Training and Research." This type of transcription is characterized by a notation system that uses symbols and graphic arrangement to indicate who is speaking when. This type of transcription preserves more language features than horizontal transcription, indicating where there were pauses, incomplete ideas, false starts, and overlaps. Below are the symbolic conventions Gilewicz and Thonus have developed.

Pause:

(.) Short pause (1–2 seconds)

(5s) Timed pause (2+ seconds)

Filled pause: um, hmm

Overlap:

Beginning shown by a right-facing bracket ([ ) placed vertically. Overlaps between participant contributions are marked using brackets aligned directly above one another. Overlaps continue until one interlocutor completes his/her utterance.

Backchannel: uh-huh, yeah, o.k., (all) right

Contributions made by other participants while the first speaker maintains the floor. Backchannels are written in lower-case (o.k.) to distinguish them from minimal responses.

Minimal response:

Uh-huh (= yes),

Uh-uh (= no),

Yeah, O.K., (All) Right

Brief responses made by participants when they have the floor.

Paralinguistic:

Nonverbal features

(( )) Additional observation—laugh, cough, sigh, etc.

^ ^ Finger snaps

> > Hand striking a surface

Analytic:

*** Indecipherable or doubtful hearing

⇒ Turns focused for analysis (Gilewicz and Thonus 29–30)

And here is a sample of a transcript using these conventions:

T: O.K.((to R)) Yeah, from listening to it, you made the transi-
tion, I think before it was different, it was kind of different, it
was hard to understand, but I think

R: uh-huh

T: you fixed it much better, and as a narrative kind of thing
it's extremely

R: uh-huh

T: believable, so that was kind of cool. So what changes did
you, did you make to it?

R: Like the transitions and   how I explain my examples
more

T: uh-huh yeah, yeah

(Gilewicz and Thonus 38).

You can see in this transcript how the speech was overlapping. Both speakers interject with verbal feedback (*uh-huh, yeah*) when the other is speaking. You can also see in line six how the transcription shows T's false start: "So what changes did you, did you make?" The difference between horizontal and close vertical are quite apparent in the two samples: one shows what the conversational partner does while listening and the other does not. Again, however, one isn't correct and the other incorrect. They just provide different information.

In addition, many researchers design their own transcription conventions. Eleanor McLellen, Kathleen McQueen, and Judith Neidig's article, "Beyond the Qualitative Interview: Data Preparation and Transcription" has really good information about developing your own transcription conventions if you chose to go this route.

About the Author

Jackie Grutsch McKinney is Director of the Writing Center and Professor of English at Ball State University in Muncie, Indiana. Her scholarship on writing center issues has appeared in key journals such as *WPA: Writing Program Administration, Writing Center Journal, Writing Lab Newsletter,* and *Praxis: A Writing Center Journal,* as well as in several writing center edited collections including *Before and After the Tutorial, Multiliteracy Centers,* and *The St. Martin's Sourcebook for Writing Tutors.* Her first book, *Peripheral Visions for Writing Centers,* won the International Writing Center Association Outstanding Book Award in 2014.

Photograph of the author by Timothy Berg. Used by permission.

Index

action research, xxi, 53, 105–117, 164
activity log, 91–92, 99, 156, 163
activity theory, 53, 135
analysis, xxi, 31, 83, 85, 88–89, 101, 104, 123–136, 144, 149, 152–153, 155, 181–182; analysis in action research, 109–110, 112–114
artifact, 61, 91– 92, 94, 95, 130, 159
audio, 28, 46, 47, 64– 66, 99, 114, 118, 125, 143, 176, 178
Auerbach, Carl, and Louise Silverstein, 131, 164
autoethnography, 90, 93–94, 96–97, 101

Babcock, Rebecca, Kellye Manning, Travis Rogers, and Courtney Goff, 15
Balester, Valerie, and James McDonald, xviii
Bell, Jim., 42, 44, 164–165
bias, 65, 101, 181
Bishop, Wendy, 65, 74–76, 84–85, 100, 102, 151, 165
Black, Laurel Johnson, 27, 41, 49, 165
Blakeslee, Ann, and Cathy Fleischer, 32, 56, 58, 98, 125, 132, 165

Bloom, Leslie Rebecca, 136, 166
Blythe, Stuart, 107, 127, 129, 133, 138, 155, 157, 164, 166
Boquet, Elizabeth, xvii, 7, 9–10, 15, 61, 166, 168
Boquet, Elizabeth, and Neal Lerner, xvii, 15
Brazeau, Alicia, 74, 85, 166
Brown, Robert, 42, 166, 171–172
Bruffee, Kenneth, 13, 166
Buck, Amber, 96, 103, 166

Calhoun, Emily, 42, 107, 108, 111–113, 116, 166
Canagarajah, Suresh, 93, 166
CAQDAS (Computer-Assisted Qualitative Data Analysis Software), 127
Carino, Peter, xviii, 73–74, 167
Carino, Peter and Doug Enders, 74
case study, 34, 53, 60, 70, 94–97, 109, 115, 130, 132
categories (analysis), 9, 40, 126, 131, 134, 142, 153, 155, 181
Charmaz, Kathy, 54, 92, 98, 135, 138, 167
Chiseri-Strater, Elizabeth and Bonnie Sunstein, 91, 100, 131
Clark, Irene Lurkis, 75, 167
close vertical transcription, 185

CPSIA information can be obtained
at www.ICGtesting.com
Printed in the USA
BVOW09s1144250517
485049BV00003B/181/P